Saving the Mail

AEI EVALUATIVE STUDIES
Marvin H. Kosters
Series Editor

Saving the Mail
How to Solve the Problems
of the U.S. Postal Service

Rick Geddes

The AEI Press

Publisher for the American Enterprise Institute

WASHINGTON, D.C.

2003

Available in the United States from the AEI Press, c/o Publisher Resources Inc., 1224 Heil Quaker Blvd., P.O. Box 7001, La Vergne, TN 37086-7001. To order, call toll free: 1-800-937-5557. Distributed outside the United States by arrangement with Eurospan, 3 Henrietta Street, London WC2E 8LU, England.

Library of Congress Cataloging-in-Publication Data
Geddes, Rick.
  Saving the mail: how to solve the problems of the U.S. Postal Service/ Rick Geddes
    p. cm.-- (AEI evaluative studies)
  Includes bibliographical references and index.
  ISBN 0-8447-4180-9 (pbk.)
    1. United States Postal Service—Management. 2. Postal Service—United States—Management I. Title. II. Evaluative studies

  HE6371 .G43 2002
  383'.4973'068—dc21

                                                                    2002038361

1 3 5 7 9 10 8 6 4 2

Printed in the United States of America

Contents

FIGURES

TABLES

Foreword

The AEI Evaluative Studies series consists of detailed empirical analyses of government programs and policies in action. Each study documents the history, purposes, operations, and political underpinnings of the program in question; analyzes its costs, consequences, and efficacy in achieving its goals; and presents proposals for reform. The studies are prepared by leading academic students of individual policy fields and are reviewed by scholars, agency officials, and program proponents and critics before publication.

The growth of public policy research in recent decades has been accompanied by a burgeoning of research and writing on proposed policies and those in the initial stages of implementation. Careful evaluation of the large base of existing programs and policies—many of them politically entrenched and no longer at the forefront of policy debate—has suffered from relative neglect. Within the government, program evaluation is typically limited to scrutiny of annual spending levels and of the number and composition of constituents who are served. Insufficient attention is devoted to fundamental questions: whether a program's social or economic goals are being accomplished, whether the goals are worthy and important, and whether they might be better achieved through alternative approaches.

The AEI series, directed by Marvin Kosters, aims to redress that imbalance. By examining government programs in action, it aims to direct more academic, political, and public attention to whether we are getting our money's worth from well-established programs and whether current "policy reform" agendas are indeed focused on issues with the greatest potential for improved public welfare.

CHRISTOPHER DEMUTH
President
American Enterprise Institute
for Public Policy Research

Acknowledgments

The study of an institution as old, as large, and as complex as the U.S. Postal Service is an inherently challenging undertaking. Even though the subject matter is clearly delineated, the amount of institutional detail is extraordinary. Developments related to postal services, both domestically and internationally, are occurring at a rapid pace. It is thus crucial to receive help and advice from others in the field to offer even a modestly comprehensive treatment.

On that score I have been exceptionally lucky. Members of the small community of postal experts have been generous with their knowledge and experience throughout the writing of this book. Although views differ on how to reform the Postal Service, or indeed on the need for reform itself, all advice was offered with the spirit of improving an important American institution.

For helpful comments and suggestions on this and earlier drafts, I am grateful to Maynard Benjamin, Jim Campbell, Bob Cohen, Murray Comarow, Michael Crew, Chris DeMuth, John Hilke, Marv Kosters, Tom Lenard, Bob McLean, Leonard Merewitz, Malin Moench, Wally Mullin, Jim Rogers, Mike Schuyler, Greg Sidak, and Robert Taub. I am thankful to all participants of the workshop on the U.S. Postal Service held at the American Enterprise Institute on August 28, 2001, for their input. Finally, I am grateful to the American Enterprise Institute for its help and support throughout the preparation of this publication.

1

Introduction

The U.S. Postal Service is America's oldest and largest public enterprise. As the Post Office, it facilitated communications between the colonies and carried messages to the furthest reaches of the nation for almost 200 years. Since 1971 it has continued to distribute mail as the U.S. Postal Service. Revenues in 2001 topped $65 billion, and more than 207 billion pieces of mail were processed.[1] Gigantic by almost any standard, it is also important internationally: it handles about 40 percent of the world's mail.[2] The Postal Service plays an important civic role as the only federal agency with which a majority of Americans interact on a daily basis.

In 2001 total postal employment was 892,005—larger than the population of Delaware and more than twice the staff of General Motors, the largest global company in terms of sales. By comparison in 1999 the U.S. population included approximately 923,000 lawyers and 837,000 automobile mechanics; the entire U.S. mining industry employed only 535,000.[3] USPS employment accounts for about 32 percent of total federal civilian employment. Until World War II the Post Office was the largest department of the federal government.

The Post Office was organized as a cabinet-level department within the executive branch of the federal government. Serious difficulties arose under that structure during the 1960s. Mail volume was increasing rapidly while antiquated equipment remained in use and operating deficits escalated. The quality of mail delivery suffered, with letter delays, erroneous deliveries, damaged parcels, and lost magazines being commonplace.[4] In October 1966, a backlog of mail exceeding 10 million pieces paralyzed Chicago's postal facility, the world's largest.[5] The President's

Commission on Postal Reorganization (better known as the Kappel commission), created by President Lyndon B. Johnson to examine the problem, identified the lack of independence of postal management, low rates of capital investment, poor working conditions, and pervasive political demands as major concerns. The commission called for the creation of an independent agency within the executive branch that would be self-financing, run like a business, and insulated from political pressure.

As a result, the Postal Reorganization Act of 1970[6] created the modern U.S. Postal Service from the Post Office in perhaps the most extensive reorganization of a federal agency.[7] Although the act had several goals, its main focus was independence for the new postal entity, both financially and managerially. Among its new powers the USPS could negotiate wages, set prices with regulatory oversight, borrow from the Treasury, and independently sue and be sued. The act exempted the USPS from federal, state, and local taxes and granted it the power of eminent domain. The postal system was to be fiscally self-sufficient by 1984.

The Timeliness of a Postal Study

Despite the importance of the Postal Service to U.S. governmental structure and to the economy, almost no rigorous empirical assessment of the act's effects has been undertaken.[8] A detailed study of its effects and consideration of reform is timely for several reasons.

First, technological developments in communications make postal reform inevitable. The growth of substitutes for letter mail in the form of the telephone, facsimiles, and particularly electronic mail suggests that postal revenues cannot be maintained at current levels without substantial rate hikes. Additional rate increases will only invite further substitution into those alternatives. Barring a return to large annual deficits and the accompanying direct taxpayer subsidies, the USPS is unlikely to remain viable for long in its present form.[9] Meaningful structural change is necessary. The General Accounting Office has recognized the situation and issued a report to the Senate Government Affairs Committee stating that the "basic business framework of the Postal Service doesn't look like it will work in the future."[10]

Second, arguments supporting the Postal Service's current organizational structure inevitably rely on subsidized mail delivery to rural areas. Yet technology has improved to such an extent, and the composition of the mail stream has changed to such an extent, that eighteenth- and nineteenth-century fears of the isolation of rural citizens absent government-provided mail are now antiquated. Rural citizens today can choose from an array of technologies that allow instant communications. Personal letters are probably not their first choice for remaining connected to the wider community. Data suggest that personal letters comprise a small fraction of the mail stream and that the composition of the mail is moving away from personal letters toward more advertising material. Moreover, recent studies suggest that the cost of serving rural and urban customers is now quite similar, so that concerns about rural customers paying dramatically more for mail delivery in a competitive market are unwarranted.

Third, industries with economic structures similar to postal services have undergone substantial organizational reform, both in the United States and internationally. Those industries share a common network structure with postal services in that they use a distribution system of lines, pipes, or routes requiring the use of public rights-of-way, typically with strong physical linkages between component parts. Network industries in the United States, including airlines, telecommunications, oil, natural gas, electricity, trucking, cable television, and railroads, have undergone meaningful regulatory reform since the mid-1970s.[11] Many of those industries must fund substantially higher fixed costs and more extensive infrastructure than postal services and are thus thought to possess more characteristics of a natural monopoly. Sufficient time has passed since deregulation in those industries to allow meaningful assessment. Such reform has generally been favorable to both consumers and producers.

Fourth, other governments have significantly altered the market structure of their postal services or have plans to do so. For example, New Zealand, Sweden, and Finland have abolished their postal monopolies.

Germany has plans to abolish its postal monopoly.[12] Australia's monopoly is limited to four times the stamp price only; that is, private firms may compete if they do not charge less than that. Canada's monopoly is three times the stamp price. The European Union has limited all European postal monopolies to five times the stamp price.

Many postal services are moving toward privatization. For example, the Dutch post is majority privately owned. Germany's immense postal service, Deutsche Post, was partially privatized on November 20, 2000, in that country's largest public offering of the year. About 29 percent of the firm was offered publicly and raised $5.6 billion, with investors applying for eight times the number of shares available.[13] Deutsche Post further commercialized by purchasing a 26 percent stake in DHL International, a leader in the global express industry. Additionally, the German government cleared the way for majority private ownership in Deutsche Post.[14]

Fifth, advances in the economics of institutions make such a study timely. Perhaps because financial economics and public finance were traditionally distinct fields in formal economic analysis, few scholars studying government corporations borrowed readily from the financial economics literature. Yet the field of corporate governance has developed to the point where it can now enhance our understanding of government-owned enterprises as well. Developments in financial economics suggest that postal reform in the United States is appropriate.

Sixth, the postal services can be used as an effective vehicle for bioterrorist attacks. Such concerns call for a reassessment of Postal Service structure. Concerns about the safety of the mail will likely accelerate substitution into alternative means of communication and will thus worsen the Postal Service's financial condition.

An Overview

This unique American institution, so significantly altered in 1970, deserves more careful academic investigation than it presently receives. This book provides just such a study. In chapter 2 I describe the details of postal structure under the Post Office and review events leading up to the 1970 Postal Reorganization Act. In the next chapter I detail the current organization of postal services as created by the act and discuss the primary justifications offered for the Postal Service's government-owned monopoly structure. Those include the universal service obligation (that is, the preservation of a cross-subsidy to rural customers) and concerns about natural monopoly. I discuss several critiques of those justifications.

I examine several measures of performance before and after the act and assess the act's effect on key variables in chapter 4. By several measures the act fostered improvements. It reduced political influence by eliminating direct congressional control over its operations. By encouraging the USPS to break even, it placed more cost of postal services onto users of mail, rather than taxpayers, and reduced the annual charge on the Treasury. Postal productivity, as measured by total factor productivity and other measures, improved.

In other ways, however, the act did not achieve its goals. It failed to reduce cross-subsidies from monopolized to competitive mail classes but instead exacerbated them. It failed to keep postal wages comparable to private sector wages, an express aim of the act. Although it did reduce the direct cost to the Treasury, it did not maintain taxpayers' equity in the Post Office but allowed it to be dissipated through recurring deficits.

I conclude that the act successfully made the USPS less dependent on politics but failed in replacing political control with effective market control. Compared with a private corporation in a competitive marketplace, the Postal Service faces inadequate control mechanisms. Reorganization could and should have been more ambitious. Chapter 5 presents the case for reform of postal services in the United States and examines the impact of technological change, the reform experience in other industries, and evidence from the growing literature on corporate governance.

I review reforms in other countries in chapter 6 . Numerous countries have significantly reformed their postal services, and important lessons can be learned from those reforms.

In chapter 7 I propose a two-step reform process, including a public offering of shares featuring employee stock ownership, with concurrent regulatory reform, and then the introduction of competition.

Those changes would more effectively achieve the Kappel commission's goals. Indeed the commission itself anticipated that more ambitious institutional change. Its introduction states:

> Were the postal system being started today, it might well be oper-
> ated by a privately-owned corporation not unlike the companies
> which operate other communication and transportation services in
> this country. We have concluded, however, that a transfer of the
> postal system to the private sector is not feasible, largely for reasons
> of financing; the Post Office should therefore continue under
> Government ownership. The possibility remains of private owner-
> ship at some future time, if such a transfer were then considered to
> be feasible and in the public interest.[15]

Such an ownership transfer is feasible and in the interest of both postal employees and the general public. Reform should be thought of as completing the work of the Postal Reorganization Act by imposing market-based, rather than political, constraints on the USPS.

Chapter 8 presents a summary and conclusions.

2

The Post Office and
the Reorganization Act

Supervision of the Post Office

Prior to the enactment of the Postal Reorganization Act of 1970, Congress directly controlled almost every facet of the operations of the Post Office as a department of the federal government.[1] A particularly important aspect was the rate structure. Control over the rate-setting process rested with Congress and the Bureau of the Budget. If the Bureau of the Budget and the White House determined that a rate change was necessary, they would call on the Office of Postal Economics within the Post Office Department to examine the issue. The Post Office was conspicuously absent from the initial impetus for a rate increase. The request would often be brought before Congress when most politically fortuitous rather than when necessary. Rate hearings might be delayed for years to avoid increases at politically inopportune times.

In hearings before Congress, a wide array of mail users would argue against rate hikes, typically relying on emotional, anecdotal evidence: As John Tierney states:

> After testimony from administration representatives, a parade of organized mail users—publishers, church groups, greeting-card manufacturers, sound-recording producers—would argue for leaving rates undisturbed or reducing the increases requested by the administration. In their presentations, the mailing interests sought to persuade committee members that widespread distribution of their products was in the public interest, and that the proposed rate

7

changes would impose on them an undue share of the total adjusted rate burden, having a devastatingly adverse effect on their operations. The hearings were filled with visions of magazines having to cease publication, direct-mail advertising companies going bankrupt, and the nation's intellectual and commercial exchange breaking down.[2]

Congress was often loath to increase rates when confronted with such stirring opposition coupled with scant organized response from the taxpayers who stood to lose from the large annual deficits that inadequate rate increases would bring. Moreover, delays in rate increases served organized mailers' interests. Delays in the 1967 rate increase, for example, collectively saved mailers $15 million each week.[3] Mailers were also effective at keeping second- and third-class mail rates low relative to first-class rates so that they could benefit from the Post Office's monopoly and thus from the relatively inelastic demand for first-class mail.

Congress also influenced the selection of postmasters. Despite the importance of those front-line managers because of their managerial skill and knowledge of local conditions, postmasters were often chosen to provide political patronage under an informal "political advisor" system.[4] That system allowed members of Congress and occasionally local party officials to choose the local postmaster. Given the substantial fringe benefits, attractive retirement packages, and job security associated with a postmaster position, it is unsurprising that those jobs were regularly used for political payoffs. The arrangement fostered more loyalty to political patrons than to the directives of central postal headquarters.

Congress also mandated numerous details of labor arrangements from wages to work assignments for particular positions. Postal unions became expert at lobbying the members of Congress who determined those arrangements. Unions exerted considerable political influence by virtue of their large size and broad geographic distribution across congressional districts. The Post Office Department was also the single most highly unionized federal organization. About 90 percent of Post Office employees belonged to a union compared with 21 percent in other federal agencies.[5] Unions used their considerable influence to lobby for higher wages, improved benefits, and greater job security.

The postal unions' success under this system was impressive. Only one postal pay bill was defeated in any House vote from 1955 to 1967.[6] When pushing through a pay bill, the unions obtained one of only two overrides of a presidential veto during the entire Eisenhower administration.[7] Numerous statistical studies, discussed below, confirm that postal workers' pay exceeded that for other workers with similar education and experience.

Congress established a variety of additional postal policies, such as the definition of mail classes, the level of capital spending by the Post Office, and the location of postal facilities. The institutional arrangements collectively led to manipulation of the Post Office for political purposes.

The corollary of almost complete congressional control over the Post Office was a profound lack of internal managerial control. The Kappel commission identified the fundamental problem:

> The organization of the Post Office as an ordinary Cabinet department guarantees that *the nominal managers of the postal service do not have authority to run the postal service.* The important management decisions of the Post Office are beyond their control and therefore cannot be made on the basis of business judgment.[8]

In addition to the problem of lack of managerial control, Post Office managers had inadequate information about postal operations. For example, postmasters did not possess information on the total cost of their operations.[9] That structure was not conducive to effective operation of the post, as subsequent events indicated.

Events Precipitating the 1970 Act

Those political incentives had unfortunate long-term consequences. Catering to large mailers' interests resulted in low revenues due to low rates, but conforming to union concerns necessitated high labor costs. Through a direct annual appropriation, taxpayers paid for the annual shortfall between revenues and costs. By consistently lobbying Congress, both organized mailers and unions obtained economic rents from taxpayers.[10] The real annual charge to the Treasury grew steadily. The Post Office deficit almost doubled from $651.7 million in 1964 to $1.1 billion in 1967.

The confluence of at least three events in the 1960s pushed the Post Office's structure to the breaking point. First, mail volumes were rising with economic growth. The total number of pieces delivered by the Post Office increased by more than 28 percent from 1960 to 1969. Second, although funding capital investment for postal delivery was rarely a top congressional priority, budgets during the 1960s were particularly inadequate. Funding for the Vietnam war and President Johnson's Great Society programs took precedence over the Post Office's capital budget. The result was limited or nonexistent capital investment and minimal technological progress.[11] Mail was still sorted by hand, and post office buildings were often physically inadequate to handle improved mechanization. Floors were sometimes too weak to handle heavy machinery, and ceilings were too low to allow large overhead conveyor networks.[12] The transportation fleet experienced an unusually high breakdown rate.

The Post Office responded by hiring more workers, but labor productivity remained low without capital improvements. Moreover, the severe personnel problems included long vacancies in postmaster positions while awaiting political appointments, low employee morale, and high rates of sick leave.

Third, changes in modes of transportation hurt the Post Office. Postal operations were designed to move mail by train, with large facilities located near train stations in downtown areas. During that time, however, railroads were rapidly declining in favor of trucks, which faced greater difficulty in reaching downtown locations.

The system reached a critical point in the 1960s. The spectacular 1966 breakdown of Chicago post office operations was not an isolated incident. A similar event occurred in Chicago in December 1963, with hundreds of thousands of Christmas parcels delayed for months.[13]

An unusual convergence of interests supported change. The Post Office itself was a major force in favor of reorganization because it would enjoy enhanced modernization and independence.[14] The business community supported reorganization because it believed that reform would lead to better service and lower rates if improved management tools were applied. Large mailers valued the improved predictability and reduced variability of rates anticipated under reorganization. The main resistance to reorganization came from organized labor, which feared a decline in its hard-won congressional influence and thus a reduction in power if collective bargaining with a continuing prohibition on strikes were adopted. Organized labor's consent was obtained through a two-part pay raise agreement and other concessions.

Goals of the Postal Reorganization Act

What was Congress trying to accomplish through reorganization? Several key goals of the Postal Reorganization Act can be identified. First, Congress envisioned improved productivity and efficiency through modern management techniques and organizational structures. The Kappel commission estimated that the Post Office could save at least 20 percent of postal costs per year if it were freed from political control and allowed to use prevailing business principles. It believed that enhanced managerial autonomy would itself improve performance, but the expected positive effect of independence on capital investment was considered particularly valuable.

Second, Congress wanted the Post Office to become financially self-sustaining. It hoped that the imposition of a break-even constraint would strengthen the Post Office's incentives for cost efficiency and reduce its reliance on government subsidies. A break-even constraint would also place the cost of postal services onto mail users rather than taxpayers generally, which would distribute costs more fairly and provide economizing incentives.

Third, rationalization of the rate structure was envisioned. As the Kappel commission noted, many decades of political rate-setting resulted in a highly irrational rate structure. It was anticipated that setting rates in accordance with accepted principles of public utility pricing would enhance both the fairness and the efficiency of postal rates.[15]

A fourth goal was reforming labor relations and working conditions. The Kappel commission found that the hiring process was extraordinarily slow, that senior appointments were politicized, that the promotion system stifled employee motivation, that employees had virtually no rewards for superior performance, that they received virtually no training, and that working environments were often shoddy. It was hoped that postal independence would address those problems.

3

The Organization of the
U.S. Postal Service

The Postal Reorganization Act of 1970, designed to achieve Congress's goals, mandated several important organizational changes. The Postal Service was to be an independent establishment of the executive branch of the federal government. The act created the independent Postal Rate Commission to oversee rate and classification changes, and to rationalize the postal rate structure. It created a corporate-like governance structure with an eleven-member board of governors. It mandated an independent personnel system, consolidated numerous trade unions, and instituted collective bargaining with binding arbitration. It required the Postal Service to break even and authorized it to borrow money and issue public bonds. The act greatly reduced direct congressional and executive control over the Postal Service but retained some minor powers of congressional oversight. But the act did not affect the Post Office's legislated monopoly over letter mail. It also did not affect uniform rates within particular weight and class categories of mail.

The immediate effects of the act were not favorable. The Postal Service was unable to meet its break-even requirement, deficits increased from $175 million in 1972 to $1.176 billion in 1976, and there was a public perception of declining service. Several factors contributed to those early problems. Inflation drove up costs, primarily through gasoline prices and rising wages, while a recession caused a decline in mail volume. Negotiated wage increases with automatic cost-of-living adjustments rapidly improved postal workers' living standards but were costly to the Postal Service.[1] The Postal Rate Commission was slow to increase rates; the first increase took seventeen months, and the second almost two years.[2] It became clear that the USPS could not continue to function as originally required by the act.

The Reorganization Act Amendments of 1976 modified the 1970 act.[3] The amendments imposed a ten-month limit on rate deliberations.[4] On receiving a decision, the governors can accept it, accept under protest, or reject.[5] Under a protest, the new rates go into effect while the governors request a modification or explanation. Additionally the amendments gave the USPS a $1 billion infusion of taxpayers' equity.

Monopoly Powers

Despite the reforms the USPS actually possesses two monopolies, one over the delivery of letters and another over the use of mailboxes.

The Delivery Monopoly. A defining feature of USPS organization is its statutory monopoly power over letter delivery, which the reorganization act did not affect. The Continental Congress, under the Ordinance of 1782, originally monopolized the delivery of letter mail in the United States. The 1782 ordinance, modeled on the British postal act of 1711, granted the post office a monopoly:

> No other person whatsoever, shall have the receiving, taking up, ordering, dispatching, sending post or with speed, carrying and delivering of any letters, packets or other dispatches from any place within these United States for hire, reward, or other profit or advantage for receiving, carrying or delivering such letters or packets respectively.[6]

More than 56 percent of the Postal Service's revenues was derived from monopolized first-class mail, while more than 24 percent was derived from partially monopolized standard mail A (formerly third-class mail).[7]

The monopoly over postal letter delivery differs critically from other utility monopolies, however, in that its scope is effectively defined by the Postal Service itself. The Private Express Statutes prohibit the private carriage of "letters or packets," and the Postal Service defines a letter as "a message directed to a specific person or address and recorded in or on a tangible object."[8] That definition, adopted by the Postal Service in 1974, differs substantially from earlier definitions and is much more expansive.[9] Such a definition leads naturally to monopolization of materials not intuitively considered letters, such as bills and advertising matter, which constitute a substantial and increasing proportion of the mail stream.[10] Moreover, the USPS can conduct searches and seizures if it suspects citizens of contravening its monopoly.

There was extensive debate about retention of the monopoly over letter delivery before and during reorganization. The Kappel commission relied on two standard justifications for retaining the delivery monopoly: (1) cross-subsidizing rural delivery and (2) natural monopoly.[11] The first is typically referred to as guaranteeing universal service and suggests that it is necessary to protect revenue from cream-skimming entry on high-volume routes, such as those within or between downtown business districts. The commission argued that it would be uneconomic to administer rates based on geography (that is, high transaction costs) and that under a uniform rate, cream-skimming on low-cost routes would leave the Postal Service with high-cost routes only. That result would drive up the Postal Service's unit costs, assuming increasing returns to scale.

Congress considered elimination of the monopoly over delivery as part of reorganization and requested that the board of governors conduct a "thorough reevaluation" of the restriction.[12] The board recommended that the prohibition be retained; the defense of the monopoly was again based partly on the theory of natural monopoly and partly on the more traditional justification of universal service.[13]

The Mailbox Monopoly. The second monopoly is a statutory monopoly over the use of private mailboxes. The Criminal Code stipulates a fine if matter on which postage has not been paid is deposited in a mailbox.[14] The Postal Service's Domestic Mail Manual requires that mailboxes "shall be used exclusively for matter which bears postage."[15]

The United States is the only country that has such a mailbox monopoly.[16] The rationales discussed below for the delivery monopoly do not apply to the mailbox monopoly. The Supreme Court, in *United States Postal Service v. Council of Greenburgh Civic Associations*, considered the constitutionality of the mailbox monopoly on the grounds of free speech. The Court came to the unappealing conclusion that postal customers must accept a monopoly over their own mailbox in return for the privilege of being subjected to the Postal Service's monopoly over letter delivery. The Court stated that "in effect, the postal customer, although he pays for the physical components of the 'authorized depository,' agrees to abide by the Postal Service's regulations in exchange for the Postal Service agreeing to deliver and pick up his mail."[17] In assessing the case, Sidak and Spulber conclude that

> although all the collected Private Express Statutes may be criticized for causing the allocative inefficiency and dynamic losses in innovation that economic analysis associates with statutory monopoly, none matches the arrogance of section 1725 in its reliance on facile arguments to imply that consumers have willingly consented to the government's monopolization of their own property.[18]

No arguments from efficiency or equity have ever been offered for the mailbox monopoly. The mailbox monopoly does have important effects in reducing competition, however, and assisting in the acquisition of additional revenues. It raises the costs to rivals of competing with the Postal Service: material may not be left in the mailbox if the customer is not home. It discourages other firms, such as utilities, from integrating into mail delivery.[19] It also discourages customers from using alternative delivery services because they must install an additional mail receptacle.

The Universal Service Rationale for the Delivery Monopoly. Although national security concerns originally motivated the delivery monopoly, as early as the 1790s government intervention in postal services in the United States became oriented toward preserving a politically beneficial cross-subsidy from the populous middle states to the relatively sparse West and South. Rural citizens received newspapers and

other information at low cost, which furthered Federalist aims to preserve and bolster the Union. George Washington was one of the first to
realize the political benefits from a monopolized post.[20] The traditional
justification for government control thus developed quite early: subsi-
dizing outlying routes with revenues from relatively populated routes.[21]

By the time of the 1845 congressional debates on the postal
monopoly, the most extensive ever conducted, private express services
were widespread. Members of Congress argued that the private expresses
would never provide service to sparsely populated areas and that the
government would consequently be left with unprofitable rural routes
and massive losses.[22] The main justification given in 1845 for legally
restricting the carriage of letters by the private expresses was again to
preserve the rural cross-subsidy.[23] That argument against competition
would be used for at least the next 150 years. In 1973 the board of
governors of the newly reorganized Postal Service stated:

> If the Private Express Statutes were repealed, private enterprise,
> unlike the Postal Service, would be free to move into the most eco-
> nomically attractive markets while avoiding markets that are less
> attractive from a business standpoint . . . . Without abandoning the
> policy of self-sufficiency and reintroducing massive subsidies, it is
> hard to see how the Postal Service could meet rate and service
> objectives in the face of cream-skimming competition against its
> major product.[24]

The Postal Service continues to invoke the cream-skimming argument. Postmaster General Marvin Runyon clearly articulated the link
between monopoly and preserving the rural cross-subsidy in 1996 when
he stated that "the Private Express Statutes provide the financial under-
pinning that allows the Postal Service to provide universal mail delivery
at a uniform postage rate for letter mail." [25]

The USPS today blames its weakening market position on
the very mandate of universal service that it champions. For example,
the 1998 *Annual Report* (Management Discussion and Outlook section)
states:

For the short term, we expect modest growth in our overall markets. However, we also expect that our competitors will further
erode our market, especially since they are not bound by the same
regulatory restrictions and government mandates that bind us.
These competitors are free to target profitable customers and sectors
of the market while avoiding others. We, however, are required to
serve everyone at the same price.

Ensuring rural service has certainly been the most durable argument
for retaining monopoly power. The inherent desirability of a uniform
rate (which along with universal service preserves the rural cross-
subsidy) is used, however, as a separate justification for monopoly
power. Without monopoly power the Postal Service argues that competition would force it to abandon uniform rates within particular weight
and class categories. Recent empirical studies suggest that may not be
the case.

Why doesn't Congress simply contract out the service to a private,
regulated monopoly that would be required to maintain universal service and uniform rates and subsidize that firm for losses incurred on rural
routes, if necessary? Commentators have responded that only by means
of government ownership are such terms assured.[26] Therefore, maintaining the cross-subsidy to low-density customers remains the principal
traditional justification for all key aspects of government involvement:
the enforced monopoly, the uniform rate, and government ownership.

The Nonexistence of Urban-Rural Cost Differentials. The above discussion assumes that serving rural customers is more costly than serving
urban ones. That view has intuitive appeal: a city carrier should be able
to serve more addresses in a given period because the proximity of
mailboxes in urban areas lowers carrier time per box. Such a view
has been fostered by historical arguments for the monopoly and by
numerous writers who have, without empirical support, taken the
rural-urban cost differential for granted.[27] It is perhaps also fostered by
the Postal Service's organizational structure, which makes a sharp distinction between rural and urban routes. City and rural mail carriers

have separate labor unions, and their compensation is determined differently.[28]

Strikingly, researchers who have examined the issue empirically conclude that urban and rural costs differ only slightly or not at all.[29] Robert Cohen, William Ferguson, and Spyros Xenakis examined those cost differences in detail, as well as the profitability of serving rural routes.[30] In terms of carrier time, they found that the average time per day per possible delivery was 1.04 minutes and 1.07 minutes for city and rural delivery, respectively. They concluded that "in the United States postal system, there is no real difference in the carrier time required to serve city and rural addresses."[31] The situation results partly because of the higher cost of serving businesses, which locate disproportionately in urban areas. Also rural residents must place a mail receptacle along the rural route traveled and must frequently use clusters of mailboxes, which lowers cost because a carrier can serve a cluster of boxes at once.[32] Finally, rural routes incur less in-house costs because there are fewer pieces per possible delivery.

Perhaps more important, Cohen, Ferguson, and Xenakis examined the profitability to the Postal Service of serving rural areas. They stated that "given the assumptions discussed above, rural delivery is remunerative and it is unlikely that it would be abandoned if the universal service requirement were eliminated."[33]

It is hard to overstate the importance of such findings for justifying the postal monopoly. If no significant urban-rural cost differences exist, no appreciable cross-subsidy exists. The cream-skimming argument for preserving the monopoly evaporates; the Postal Service would not be left with unprofitable routes even if competitive entry occurred only on urban routes. There is no reason to believe that rural areas would be unserved without the universal service requirement. Indeed, Cohen and his colleagues concluded that "it is likely that if the universal service requirement were eliminated, even the most sparsely populated rural areas would receive service."[34] Without significant urban-rural cost differentials, the link between government-enforced monopoly and universal service is broken, and the key justification for the delivery monopoly vanishes.

Critiques of Urban-Rural Cost Differentials. The available empirical studies indicating no significant urban-rural cost differentials are convincing. But they may not convince some readers who continue to view the cross-subsidy to rural customers as important. Several critiques of the universal service rationale for the postal monopoly remain even in the presence of significant urban-rural cost differentials.

First, elementary economics implies that rural areas are unlikely to receive no postal delivery whatsoever if the cross-subsidy were eliminated. Firms would instead serve outlying areas but charge them more if the benefits of the cost differential exceeded the expense of implementing a graduated pricing scheme. The maintenance of universal service is consistent with a variety of rate structures. Uniform rates and universal service have become confused in discussions of postal reform. Importantly, universal service could be maintained while rural service remained *affordable,* but perhaps not at uniform rates. Rather than becoming isolated, rural customers might pay the greater cost of delivery to them to the extent that those higher costs exist. Universal service simply does not imply a uniform rate.

Rural customers would likely receive competitive service. Many alternative delivery services, including United Parcel Service, Federal Express, and newspaper and circular deliveries, frequently cover rural routes; substantial competition would arise to meet demand.[35] Delivery networks to service those areas already exist and could easily incorporate letter delivery through contracts. Moreover, contracts could be competitively awarded; that process would eliminate the need for statutory monopoly. A recent study by Harvard economist Andre Shleifer singled out the Postal Service as a canonical case of how contracting could be used effectively:

> A common argument for government ownership of the postal service is to enable the government to force the delivery of mail to sparsely populated areas, where it would be unprofitable to deliver it privately. From the contractual perspective, this argument is weak. The government can always bind private companies that compete for a mail delivery concession to go wherever

the government wants, or it can alternatively regulate these companies when entry is free. It cannot be so difficult to write the appropriate contract or regulation; after all, the government now *tells* the U.S. Postal Service where it wants the mail to be delivered.[36]

Such a delivery concession is already operating through a licensing mechanism in the United Kingdom and other countries, as discussed in chapter 6.

The second critique of the universal service justification is that private firms facing competition would likely provide universal service even if they lost money on certain routes. The provision of universal service by a private firm, even under competition, is an important business asset. Firms have an incentive to maintain a universal delivery network in order to guarantee consumers the option of sending material to all addresses. All else being equal, consumers prefer a firm that maintains a universal network to one that does not. That finding is consistent with United Parcel Service and Federal Express maintaining ubiquitous delivery networks even in the presence of competition.[37]

Third, maintaining universal service does not necessarily mean the maintenance of six-day delivery to all addresses or indeed any particular aspect of delivery quality. Routes that are unprofitable to serve six days per week may become profitable with less frequent service.[38] That is, *universal service* may actually mean providing excessively frequent service to addresses on unprofitable routes. Under competition deliveries would instead be made at an economically efficient frequency.

Fourth, and perhaps most important, no logical link exists between the preservation of universal service and the need for legally enforced monopoly. If guaranteeing universal service is costly, there is no reason why that cost must be funded through monopoly rents from urban delivery. Indeed the enforcement of entry barriers may be the most costly way conceivable to fund universal service. The enormous social costs of legally enforced monopoly are well known and are discussed in chapter 5. As James Campbell notes, the costs of universal service could instead be funded through a modest tax on delivery companies:

In sum, it appears that a relatively small sales tax, on the order of a few percent or less, on the delivery of all small documents, administered by an agency such as the Postal Rate Commission, will cover whatever may be the costs of maintaining universal service for all retail letters at a uniform rate. Such a mechanism would cost the mailing public an amount on the order of zero to a few hundreds of million of dollars per year. This approach would represent a great savings over the current postal monopoly, which costs the mailing public monopoly profits on the order of ten or more billions of dollars per year.[39]

To recap, there are several criticisms of the universal service rationale for the delivery monopoly. First, available empirical evidence suggests that no significant cost differences exist in providing urban and rural mail delivery; monopoly is unnecessary to ensure universal service. Second, if cost differences did exist, universal service would be provided without a monopoly, but private firms facing competition would simply charge different rates. That is, universal service does not imply uniform rates. Third, private firms facing competition have a market incentive to provide universal service because it is valuable. Fourth, universal service does not imply a particular frequency of mail delivery or level of delivery quality. Firms facing competition may be willing to provide universal service but make deliveries less frequently than in urban areas. Fifth, the need to enforce a delivery monopoly does not follow logically from a desire to guarantee universal service. If ensuring universal service is both desirable and costly, those costs can be funded through various mechanisms other than monopoly rents. Legally enforced monopoly may be the most socially costly method of funding universal service.

The Natural Monopoly Rationale for the Delivery Monopoly. The second major argument for the postal monopoly is that postal services are a "natural monopoly."[40] Rather than defending the monopoly at the time of its codification in 1845, however, natural monopoly theory was developed much later as an ex post rationale for intervention in network industries generally. Natural monopoly theory provides a modern defense of government ownership and monopolization of the postal industry.[41]

In its report to Congress, the Board of Governors of the Postal Service argued that the prohibitions on private carriage must be retained and, in addition to relying on the traditional universal service rationale, appealed to the concept of natural monopoly.[42] Commentators continue to assert that at least the local delivery network exhibits natural monopoly characteristics.[43]

Natural monopoly is said to exist when a single firm can supply a good at lower cost than can two or more firms.[44] The notion is intimately related to that of economies of scale. Scale economies are present if the firm's average costs decline as output increases.[45] If the firm produces a single product, then economies of scale throughout the entire range of output are a sufficient condition for natural monopoly.[46]

According to traditional natural monopoly theory, achieving least-cost production (that is, productive efficiency) entails the existence of only one firm operating in the industry and thus requires legally protected territorial monopolies. Because the check of competition has been removed, however, the monopoly firm must be regulated (or government-owned) to prevent price gouging, to ensure that it produces at the correct level of output (that is, allocative efficiency), and to guarantee that it receives only a reasonable return on its investment.[47] Government intervention ensures both productive and allocative efficiency and thus improves on market outcomes.

Critiques of the Natural Monopoly Rationale. Perhaps the most important critique of natural monopoly as a justification for legally enforced monopoly is its lack of internal inconsistency. There is no need to prevent entry if a firm is truly a natural monopolist. The firm can always force out rivals by expanding output and lowering prices. In critiquing the board of governor's 1973 report, George Priest states:

> The Governors give the impression in the arguments they marshal,
> that their defense of the statutes establishing the monopoly (the private express statutes) rests on the theory of natural monopoly. The

private express statutes, they suggest, are unobjectionable because the postal industry possesses the characteristics of decreasing average costs. But the theory of natural monopoly is inapposite. The theory might explain economic evolution that led (naturally) to monopoly, but the Governors are not defending such evolution; it never occurred. The Governors are defending the necessity of a legal prohibition on entry into the industry, and for that, theory provides no support. If an industry truly possesses natural monopoly characteristics, there is no need to prohibit entry. By definition the dominant firm will always be able to underbid, and thus eliminate, any potential competitor. In fact, the discussion of natural monopoly in the Report is a ruse, for the Governors themselves accept this analysis.[48]

There are additional reasons why scholars have become dissatisfied with natural monopoly theory as a justification for intervention in industry generally. Because natural monopoly justifications for the postal monopoly occasionally resurface, it is useful to recount those reasons. First, economists have presented evidence suggesting other powerful motives for intervention besides correction of natural monopoly. For example, politically influential groups may seek government regulation to acquire economic rents from less influential groups.[49]

Second, the approach has been criticized because it lacks a realistic mechanism for translating market failure into regulation. That is, no framework taking into account the rational behavior of politicians, regulators, or interest groups would translate the demand for corrective intervention into the desired outcomes. For example, natural monopoly theory implies that regulators ignore the interests of producers (a powerful pressure group) and concern themselves only with the interests of consumers. Natural monopoly theory is thus highly prescriptive or normative in character.[50]

Third, a substantial body of research—beginning with Demsetz's seminal 1968 article, "Why Regulate Utilities?"—directly confronts the logical consistency of the natural monopoly rationale for regulation.[51] Demsetz showed that the existence of a single producer in the market need not lead to monopolistic pricing. Competitors can bid for the right to serve the market. Demsetz demonstrated that the threat of *potential entry* can discipline markets that have few, or only one, producer actually in the market. Competition for mail delivery concessions, as discussed above, illustrates that notion.

The concept of potential competition has substantially influenced economics. It was rigorously analyzed in a body of work known as contestability theory. Robert Willig first examined the notion in detail in 1980 by applying it to postal markets, which he found to be highly contestable. A series of papers, including those by William Baumol and Robert Willig,[52] as well as Elizabeth Bailey and John Panzar, developed it further.[53] The inquiry led to a benchmark idealized state termed a *perfectly contestable market*. As Baumol and his colleagues state, "A perfectly contestable market is defined as one in which entry and exit are easy and costless, which may or may not be characterized by economies of scale or scope, but which has no entry barriers."[54] That work emphasized the ease of entry into and exit from a market, rather than cost conditions.[55] It called into question the original notion of natural monopoly and therefore the justification for monopoly rate-of-return style regulation. The assets required for letter delivery, such as trucks and buildings for sorting, are easily adaptable to other uses; the costs of entry and exit are likely to be relatively low. Even a naturally monopolistic postal service would not justify a legally enforced delivery monopoly because postal markets are likely to be highly contestable.

Fourth, many regulated firms produce more than one product. Utilities produce both peak and off-peak power, telephone companies provide both local and long-distance phone service, and the Postal Service delivers several classes of mail. Economies of scale are neither necessary nor sufficient for an industry to be considered a natural monopoly in the multiproduct case. The existence of economies of scale in the local delivery network is insufficient to prove that postal markets are naturally monopolistic.

Collectively that literature led to a widespread change in the acceptance of natural monopoly as a rationale for government intervention in industry.[56] Whatever the original validity of such claims, technological developments have made the natural monopoly rationale for government intervention in postal services more dubious (see chapter 5).

"Suspension" of the Delivery Monopoly. Unsurprisingly the Postal Service vigilantly defends its monopoly powers. Referring to a General Accounting Office study that considered relaxation of the Private Express Statutes, the *Washington Post* reported that "the postmaster general also said the GAO 'seriously underestimates the magnitude of revenue losses that would occur across all classes of mail if Congress were to remove the statutes.' Those comments indicate that Runyon, like his predecessors, will probably fight efforts to ease the agency's mail monopoly."[57] The Postal Service's desire to maintain its monopoly is unsurprising politically. It allows the Postal Service to secure and redistribute economic rents to politically influential groups and remain politically, if not economically, viable.

More interestingly the USPS in 1973 assumed the power to "suspend" the monopoly at will for certain types of messages. As George Priest states:

> In the 1973 Report the Governors announce for the first time that they possess and that they will exercise the authority to suspend the private express statutes at their discretion. No Postmaster General has ever claimed the power to repeal or to "suspend" the private express statutes by administrative order. But the Governors have discovered an obscure postal regulation which will allow them, with sympathetic interpretation, to surrender bits and pieces of their exclusive grant in ways to preserve the substance of the monopoly.[58]

The suspension power allows the USPS itself to decide who falls under its monopoly. As James C. Miller writes:

> Through its ability to define a "letter," the Postal Service is in the enviable position of being able to determine the extent of its own monopoly. While the service has "suspended" its monopoly for certain letters (such as time-sensitive materials), it has also expanded its

monopoly by defining letters to include bills, receipts, IBM cards, magnetic tapes, and other business documents. Typically, as new services such as express mail have developed, the Postal Service has first asserted that these services fall within its monopoly and then announced a suspension of the monopoly with respect to *some* aspects of the new service.[59]

It remains unclear whether Congress ever gave the Postal Service authority to suspend the postal monopoly. As James C. Campbell writes:

To mitigate opposition to its new definition of *letter*, the Postal Service also issued regulations which purported to "suspend" the postal monopoly. These "suspensions" created administrative exceptions from the postal monopoly for newspapers, magazines, checks (when sent between banks), data processing materials (under certain circumstances), urgent letters, international remail, etc. While the suspensions have prevented politically powerful mailers from petitioning for Congressional review of the postal monopoly, it appears clear that, as a matter of law, Congress has never authorized the Postal Service to suspend the postal monopoly. As statutory authority for these suspensions, the Postal Service cites an 1864 postal act. However, it is apparent from even a superficial reading of the legislative history of the act that this provision was never intended to confer authority to suspend the postal monopoly.[60]

Gregory Sidak and Daniel Spulber discussed suspensions of the postal monopoly in detail.[61] Exceptions include the obvious, such as "letters accompanying cargo" and "letters of the carrier" (which encompass interoffice correspondence) and more importantly "letters by special messenger," as well as "extremely urgent letters."

Such "suspension" behavior is unintelligible and counterproductive according to the natural monopoly justification for intervention because relaxation of the monopoly power would increase costs by inviting competition. If the monopoly were necessary to maintain rural service, suspensions would also appear to be counterproductive because they reduce revenue. Politically, however, the mitigation of opposition to the postal monopoly is critical.[62] Rather than using dollars directly to mitigate opposition, the USPS instead grants wealth through access to lucrative overnight markets. Firms such as United Parcel Service, DHL, and Federal Express, which might otherwise constitute well-organized opposition, are assuaged by this selective entry.[63] Through the suspension authority, the USPS is able to micromanage its monopoly power to mitigate opposition. Although the continuation of the monopoly and its selective suspension are not consistent with the prevailing public-interest arguments for them, they are consistent with the redistribution of economic rents to politically influential groups.

The mailbox and delivery monopolies, important aspects of the Postal Service's institutional structure, do not serve a socially beneficial purpose. They are instead socially detrimental. They exist not to enhance economic efficiency, but to redistribute economic rents to particular influential political constituencies. In particular, small, highly organized groups are likely to benefit at the expense of larger groups facing higher organization costs. A novel example illustrates the point.

Under old postal regulations, poultry farmers could airmail newborn chicks to their customers. The Postal Service would arrange for transportation on a commercial airliner. Because of the special care required in flight and the low rates paid, airlines lost money on airmailed chicks. Northwest Airlines announced that it would stop accepting airmailed chicks as mail and instead accept them only as cargo, for which it charges higher rates. A small, highly organized political pressure group, Birdshippers of America, organized a lobbying campaign to force the airlines to continue to accept the chicks as mail, that is, to continue to subsidize their delivery. Congress responded by inserting a provision in an appropriations bill stating that the Postal Service can force an airline to carry "day old poultry and such other live animals as postal regulations allow" at mail rates.[64] The change illustrates how the Postal Service's legal structure can be used to redistribute wealth from less well-organized groups (the airlines) to better-organized groups (the bird shippers). The monopoly powers are a manifestation of the phenomenon, writ large.

The Uniform Rate

The USPS, as before restructuring, is required to provide universal service within the United States at uniform rates for weight-class categories for the majority of mail it delivers regardless of distance or customer density.[65] For example, as of June 30, 2002, any letter weighing less than 1 ounce will be delivered first-class anywhere in the country for 37 cents. Given the state of debate on the uniform rate, it is useful to consider two cases: (1) where there are no significant differences in the cost of serving rural compared with urban customers, as recent evidence indicates,[66] and (2) where rural service is more costly than urban service.

Under case 1 an enforced uniform rate is difficult to understand. If the uniform rate were repealed, customers would pay the cost of delivery to them, which may or may not be higher in rural areas. Here the Postal Service's standard defense of the uniform rate, to protect rural delivery, appears to be inadequate.

The USPS has, however, attempted to justify the uniform rate further on what appear to be the grounds of transactions cost, independent of any urban-rural cost differences. As George Priest stated: "The Postal Service must charge uniform rates. The Postal Service has found, according to the Governors, that it is only practicable to set rates 'according to simple, published formulas of great generality.'"[67] Moreover, "the Governors further assert that with any varied pricing structure 'regulatory red tape' will proliferate and the public will become confused."[68] Transactions cost arguments also appear to be at the bottom of the Kappel commission's cream-skimming argument against nonuniform rates: "It would probably be uneconomic for the Post Office to meet competition by offering a reduced rate for such service because of the additional costs of administering a rate scheme split along geographic lines."[69]

Transactions cost arguments for an enforced uniform rate are problematic. Market forces, in the absence of monopoly prohibitions, naturally act to conserve on transaction costs. If the reduction in confusion brought about by uniform rates actually offset higher costs due to suboptimal pricing, then competitive private companies would have the incentive to adopt uniform rates. There would be no need to enforce them by law.

Additional evidence suggests that enforced uniform rates within a class are not necessary to control transactions costs or to avoid customer confusion. The USPS itself abandons uniform rates for its standard mail B parcel post business and prices by zones for that service. If there is a public-interest justification to enforce uniform rates in the other mail classes, it is unclear why those considerations do not apply to standard mail B. Finally, if the urban-rural cost differences are small as Cohen and his colleagues indicated, abandonment of the uniform rate requirement would be unlikely to lead to a substantial change in rates. The uniform rate requirement thus dispenses no public benefit.

In case 2 significant differences exist in the cost of serving rural versus urban customers by assumption. Combined with monopoly power, the difference implies that a uniform rate creates an intraclass cross-subsidy from urban to rural customers. Without the monopoly, private competitors would enter on all routes where price exceeds unit cost, skim the cream off the most profitable routes, and leave the Postal Service with only the least profitable customers. That is, because profit-maximizing firms will compete until prices equal cost, uniform rates would have to be abandoned if the Private Express Statutes were repealed and entry were allowed on all routes. The Postal Service, which apparently assumes that significant urban-rural cost differences exist, insists that monopoly must be retained to facilitate uniform rates.

Even if such cost differences exist, it is difficult to appreciate how this policy is consistent with the public interest. Aside from the wide variety of inefficiencies associated with legally enforced monopoly itself, the social loss from cross-subsidy induced by uniform rates has been understood for more than half a century.[70] Such rates result in overuse of postal services on high-cost routes and underuse on low-cost routes.

Given the availability of electronic mail, facsimile machines, lower long-distance telephone rates and plane fares, and lower-cost overnight delivery services, the claim that rural customers would become isolated if uniform rates were abandoned and they paid their true cost of delivery today rings hollow. It is doubtful that rural customers would receive no service if the uniform rate were replaced; they would instead pay the true cost of serving them. No remaining public-interest rationale exists for the continuance of that pricing scheme.

As with monopoly power, an alternative explanation for the uniform rate focuses on the private parties that stand to benefit. The Postal Service can influence the amount of economic rent that various groups receive through the rate structure. Say that serving urban customers costs 32 cents per letter, while serving rural customers costs 37 cents per letter. A uniform rate of 34 cents results in a tax of 2 cents per letter on urban customers to provide rural customers with a subsidy of 3 cents. A cross-subsidy from urban to rural customers exists.[71]

A uniform rate-pricing structure in the presence of cost differences is consistent with such politically beneficial rent redistribution within a class of mail. Under the assumption of significant urban-rural cost differences, the preservation of rent redistribution through cross-subsidy provides an explanation for USPS behavior toward relaxation of the monopoly statutes as well as the uniform rate. Both are necessary to preserve cross-subsidies.

Government Ownership

Ownership form is one of the most contentious issues surrounding postal organization. Consistent with the Kappel commission's recommendations, under the Postal Reorganization Act the USPS was said to be "commercialized" but remained wholly government-owned.[72] The federal government effectively retains monopoly ownership of the Postal Service.

Kappel Commission's Arguments for Government Ownership. The Kappel commission, though conceding the superiority of private ownership, suggested unusual reasons for retaining monopoly government ownership:

> If the postal system had begun after the country had reached an advanced stage of technological, social and economic development,

it would in all likelihood have emerged as a private industry suit-
ably regulated to ensure satisfactory service levels and fair prices.
Most members of this Commission would favor an investor-owned
postal system.

We recognize, however, that formidable barriers stand in the
way of a transfer of the existing postal system to private ownership.
The Post Office has had two hundred years as a Government operation. Time has nurtured the attitude that the postal service must be
a Government responsibility.

Private operation, furthermore, presumes a buyer and a seller. It
is clear that an organization with the Post Office's earnings record
would not attract investors. Our contractors estimated the current
appraised value of postal fixed assets at approximately $1.7 billion.
That figure, together with the $5 billion modernization requirement
estimated by the Post Office, would make for formidable stock and
bond issues. It is highly improbable that issues of the size necessary
to complete financing within a reasonable period could be undertaken in these times.[73]

Aside from the unsatisfying assertion of a public perception of
inevitable government ownership, the commission issues two arguments
questioning the feasibility of placing ownership in private hands.[74] First,
the Post Office's earnings record would not attract investors. Second, the
size of the issue is too large for the capital markets to absorb.

The first argument ignores the fact that the Postal Service's poor
earnings record is itself a function of government ownership. No
well-defined residual claimants exist under government ownership.
Residual claimants are those who have property rights to the net cash
flow of an organization, such as stockholders in a privately owned,
public traded corporation or the partners of a partnership. Without a
well-defined group of residual claimants, there is no incentive to increase
the size of net cash flows through cost minimization and revenue
maximization. The capital markets would likely take into account the

change in incentives brought about by private ownership in pricing its shares. Additionally the value of the Postal Service is a direct function of the institutional arrangements made before its public offering, for example, regarding pension liabilities and health care costs. There is no reason why those arrangements cannot be made attractive to investors. Moreover, the enhanced proceeds from the stock offering could be used to offset the cost to taxpayers of those institutional arrangements.

The commission's second argument against private ownership is that postal services in the United States are too large for the capital markets to absorb. Given today's global capital markets, that argument seems intuitively false. Moreover, there is no reason why public offerings cannot be undertaken in installments over years if necessary. Deutsche Post's successful large offering calls both contentions into question, as investors applied for eight times more than the number of shares actually available.[75] That success suggests that such an offering is feasible and that investors view postal shares as profitable.

Those appear to be the Kappel commission's only arguments against privatization, a strategy it otherwise clearly preferred. Its advocacy of transferable ownership would likely have been stronger had the scholarship summarized in chapter 5 been available.

Strikingly an alternative justification provided by political scientists for retaining government ownership again appears to be ensuring universal delivery, that is, guaranteeing service to low-density customers. John Tierney summarizes that view:

> The interesting question here is why the federal government of the United States has sometimes chosen the government corporation as its strategy of intervention rather than employing some sort of subsidy, tax expenditure, or coercive regulation. The typical answers involve three sorts of problems: *risk*, where private entrepreneurs do not see sufficient possibility of return on investment (as in the case of the Synthetic Fuels Corporation); *scope*, where the amount of capital raised and the area of activities to be covered are great (as in the case of large infrastructure investments such as the projects of the Tennessee Valley Authority); and *service-maintenance*,

where not only are economic returns not particularly promising, but alternative sources of service are uncertain. The last category would encompass Amtrak, the Postal Service, and the like.[76]

Because no one questions the adequacy of service in urban areas in a de-monopolized market, the service-maintenance argument is only relevant for rural areas. The empirical work discussed above calls that argument into question by suggesting that rural routes would be served even without enforced monopoly.

Political Benefits of Government Ownership. Several alternative reasons for retaining government ownership have little to do with rural service maintenance per se but rather allow the Postal Service to accumulate and redistribute economic rents generally. Government ownership means that the Postal Service is statutorily released from the pursuit of profits; that release gives it a legal and political shield to dissipate rents.[77] Government ownership permits USPS equity, which represents taxpayers' investment, to be dissipated through deficits. The Post Office ran deficits continuously before the act.[78] The Postal Service was required to become self-financing, that is, to break even, as discussed below.[79] However, it ran deficits for twenty of the thirty years between 2001 and the act's implementation.[80] The Postal Service's financial problems do not appear to be abating.

Although an improvement relative to pre-act years, the performance is hardly attractive to private investors. Since 1970 the USPS has depleted large amounts of taxpayers' equity. It started operations in 1971 with positive initial equity of $1.7 billion and was provided an additional $1 billion through the 1976 amendments.[81] Taxpayers' equity nevertheless reached a low in fiscal 1994 of minus $5.961 billion.[82] Government ownership allows equity depletion and absolution from paying investors a rate of return. The creation of transferable residual claims would constrain the Postal Service to provide investors with a positive expected rate of return.

Government ownership of the Postal Service facilitates rent accumulation in several additional ways. First, government ownership allows borrowing from the Federal Financing Bank.[83] The federal government guarantees that debt.[84] The Postal Service can thus obtain additional funding when private credit markets would not be forthcoming. Such preferential borrowing has likely saved the USPS billions of dollars in interest costs since its inception.[85]

The Postal Service enjoys a host of exemptions and privileges by virtue of government ownership. Each saves the USPS a substantial amount annually. The USPS is exempt from federal, state, and local income taxes.[86] It is exempt from many licensing and zoning laws. It is exempt from many financial reporting requirements.[87] It has the power of eminent domain. It has federal priority for the payment of debts from bankrupt estates.[88] Those cost savings may assist the USPS in maintaining universal service, but organized interest groups such as labor unions and large, well-organized mailers probably capture some benefits as well.

In sum, no plausible public interest rationales exist for retaining government ownership of the Postal Service. Government ownership does, however, allow the Postal Service to secure and redistribute a significant amount of economic value.

The Postal Rate Commission

To regulate that government-owned monopoly, the 1970 act created the Postal Rate Commission: the president appoints its five members with advice and consent of the Senate.[89] The commission recommends postal rates and classifications to the board after the USPS has requested a rate change.[90] The commission is required by the act to take the following criteria into account when evaluating proposed rates:[91]

1. The establishment and maintenance of a fair and equitable schedule.
2. The value of the mail service actually provided each class or type of mail service to both the sender and the recipient, including but not limited to the collection, mode of transportation, and priority of delivery.
3. The requirement that each class of mail or type of mail service bear the direct and indirect postal costs attributable to that class

or type plus that portion of all other costs of the Postal Service reasonably assignable to such class or type.

4. The effect of rate increases upon the general public, business mail users, and enterprises in the private sector of the economy engaged in the delivery of mail matter other than letters.

5. The available alternative means of sending and receiving letters and other mail matter at reasonable costs.

6. The degree of preparation of mail for delivery into the postal system performed by the mailer and its effect upon reducing costs to the Postal Service.

7. Simplicity of structure for the entire schedule and simple, identifiable relationships between the rates or fees charged the various classes of mail for postal services.

The act also requires the USPS to break even. Its fees and rates are to produce total revenues that (including the authorized subsidy payments from the Treasury) equal total operating costs.[92] Therefore, with the exception of temporary subsidies, the act imposed a budget constraint. To help achieve that goal and enhance capitalization, the act authorized the Postal Service to borrow money and issue public bonds to finance postal buildings, mechanization, and modernization. The USPS can borrow from the Federal Financing Bank within statutory limits, and taxpayers guarantee its debt. The limit on borrowing is $2 billion in any one year for capital purposes and $1 billion for operating purposes. Total debt outstanding cannot exceed $15 billion.[93] Rates allowing the USPS to break even while reflecting those criteria may be laudable, but the Postal Rate Commission was not granted adequate authority to achieve those goals.

Powers of the Postal Rate Commission. Although the Postal Rate Commission appears at first blush to be similar in structure to a public utility commission regulating a privately owned utility, its powers are weaker. First, the commission was established not to set postal rates per se but to *recommend* rates to the board after a rate change request from the Postal Service.[94] A recommended change in a rate proposal is sent to the board for reconsideration, and the board can overrule the commission provided it is unanimous.[95] In an analogously regulated utility, a firm's board of directors would have the power to overturn the rate decisions of its state public utility commission and institute its own desired rates. The board of governors has used that power. It overruled the commission in 1981 and raised first-class rates to 20 cents after being thrice rebuffed by the commission.[96] More recently the board voted unanimously to overrule the commission and implement rate increases effective July 1, 2001.[97]

Second, the commission is weak because of government ownership itself. It cannot reduce the wealth of stockholders by reducing rates or by threatening to do so. A public utility commission can reduce equity values by refusing to raise rates, by raising them slowly, or by reducing them.[98] That important power normally places substantial pressure on managers in a private firm because private ownership facilitates strong links between shareholder wealth and the interests of managers, which are eliminated by government ownership.

Third, the structure of the rate-making process prevents the commission from effectively imposing a revenue constraint. The commission must take the Postal Service's costs as given and try to allocate those costs across the various mail classes. Denying rate increases can reduce equity under private ownership. The Postal Service, however, can simply claim inability to meet its costs, such as payroll, and force the commission to either raise its rates or risk overdrafts.[99] The commission consequently has little power to constrain the costs of the USPS, which are the main determinant of rates. The break-even constraint is thus considerably softer than the revenue constraint of a private competitive firm.

Fourth, the commission does not have the power to regulate the quality of postal services.[100] The Postal Service itself can determine critical variables, such as the number of deliveries per day and per week, and the speed of deliveries.[101] The USPS has latitude for rent redistribution on that important additional margin.

Fifth, the commission is weak because it lacks adequate information on Postal Service operations. The Postal Service is positioned to have the best information on its operations, and the commission depends on the Postal Service to provide that information. As former Postal Rate Commission Chairman Clyde S. DuPont stated:

> Part of the problem too, is the lack of any *explicit* statutory authority . . . to prescribe or require the Postal Service to collect particular types of data. Although our discovery powers are generally sufficient to permit us to test and clarify evidence presented in our proceedings, the service has treated the actual collection of data as its exclusive domain. It reserves the design of its statistical systems and the data to be released as a matter of unilateral discretion. . . . Thus the commission and the parties to our proceedings have been tied to the data the Postal Service is willing and able to make available.[102]

The situation contrasts sharply with the information disclosure requirements faced by a privately owned regulated utility, which includes subpoenas and audits. USPS control over its information likely weakens the commission's ability to regulate it properly.

Postal scholars have noted that the commission's weakness essentially allows the Postal Service to price in an unconstrained manner. Though normally sympathetic to the Postal Service's legal structure, John Tierney stated, "It hardly seems an acceptable situation that a government agency enjoying a monopoly over certain of its services has the ultimate power to put into effect whatever rates it chooses."[103]

It is instructive to examine in detail the authority and mandate that the Postal Rate Commission possesses to control a particularly contentious issue in postal pricing: the relative institutional burden placed on various classes of mail to fund the Postal Service's costs. The courts' interpretation of the act on this issue further indicates the Postal Rate Commission's weakness.

The Postal Rate Commission and Cross-Subsidization. A key objective of Congress in creating the commission and its rate-making criteria was to shift the cost of postal services from government to "all users of mail" and to eliminate cross-subsidies between classes of mail. A more specific aim of Congress was to reduce the burden on first-class mail in the name of fairness.[104] Both researchers and courts have noted that first-class mail has traditionally subsidized other classes. For example, in *National Association of Greeting Card Publishers v. United States Postal Service,* 569 F.2d. 570, at 587 (D.C. Cir. 1976) the U.S. Court of Appeals for the District of Columbia Circuit stated, "Discrimination in postal rate making in favor of certain preferred classes of mail and to the great disadvantage of first class mail has long been a part of our postal system."[105]

The critical section of the act relating to prevention of that cross-subsidy mandates "that each class of mail or type of mail service bear the direct and indirect postal costs attributable to that class or type plus that portion of all other costs of the Postal Service reasonably assignable to such class or type."[106] That section appears intended to move postal pricing away from value-of-service, or inverse-elasticity, pricing toward cost-based rates. Inverse-elasticity pricing applies to firms selling several products or services. It results in the highest markups over marginal cost being assigned to those products or services displaying the lowest elasticities.

Despite the well-known economic efficiency of inverse-elasticity, or Ramsey, pricing,[107] the elasticities incorporated must be those arising from competitive conditions, under which demand reflects willingness to pay, not those induced by statutory monopoly.[108] Ramsey pricing will result in misallocation of resources when the elasticities used in its calculation are distorted by monopoly.[109] Specifically it will result in excessively high prices being charged to services in which elasticities are artificially low due to monopoly and in excessively low prices for services facing competition. It is therefore highly desirable in the case of legally mandated monopoly that the firm use cost-based, rather than inverse-elasticity, rates. Indeed the Court of Appeals for the District of Columbia Circuit ruled that the act disallowed inverse-elasticity pricing in favor of cost-of-service pricing and strongly reiterated that position in 1978.[110]

In 1983, however, the Supreme Court overturned the D.C. Circuit and essentially found that the act contained no specific methods for allocating institutional costs that the commission need follow.[111] The Court decided that the commission could assign direct costs on the basis of cost of service and assign remaining costs on the basis of other factors. The decision leaves the USPS free to allocate about half its costs according to what the market will bear.[112] The decision essentially allows it to "tax" letter mail to subsidize other mail classes, as noted by authorities in postal matters. For example, the Postal Rate Commission's chief administrative law judge, Seymour J. Wenner, who acted as hearing examiner in the first two rate cases after reorganization, stated:

> The Postal Service has become a tax-collecting agency, collecting money from first-class mailers to distribute to other favored classes. Every time a person pays 10 cents to mail a first-class letter, he is paying his appropriate share of residual costs, and in addition, he is contributing almost 2 cents to pay the costs of other services.[113]

It appears that the commission not only lacks the economic tools to prevent cross-subsidy from monopolized to competitive classes but lacks the legal mandate as well.

The Board of Governors

The Kappel commission recommended, and the act mandated, a corporate-like board of governors. The board has eleven members, nine appointed by the president with advice and consent of the Senate. Those nine appoint the postmaster general, and those ten then appoint the deputy postmaster general.[114] The postmaster general, however, is not a full governor and cannot vote on the acceptance or rejection of the Postal Rate Commission's recommended decisions. Since the Kappel commission explicitly intended its reforms to make the Postal Service more businesslike and referred to this structure as a "public corporation," a comparison with the board of a privately owned corporation is invited.

A crucial question is to whom the postal board of governors should be accountable. The answer is obvious for the board of directors of a privately owned (but publicly traded) corporation. That board has a fiduciary duty to make decisions in the interests of the firms' stockholders. The analogous group for the Postal Service is its citizen-owners.[115]

There are reasons to believe that the board of governors is much less accountable to the Postal Service's owners than the board of a private corporation is to its owners. Owners directly elect the board of directors in a private firm. Power over compensation plans, monitoring of top managers, and ratification of new projects were delegated to the board.[116] Owners, however, typically retain control rights over such decisions as board membership, audits, takeovers, and new stock issues.

The act achieved the objective of giving the managers of the Postal Service greater autonomy. Owners, however, were not given any additional control rights over the board and may have less internal control than before. Because they cannot directly vote board members out, owners cannot remove board members who are not effectively controlling the firm's decision process. Consequently board members who perform ineffectively have little risk of being ousted. Owners can elect a U.S. president only in the tenuous hope that amid all his other responsibilities, he will monitor the board to serve the interests of owners. Presidential appointment of board members has two additional levels of control, or agency, problems relative to a private firm: one between the owners and the president and a second between the president and the board. The new, powerful board has no incentive to behave in the interests of owners.

Stockholders do possess a fundamental power: the ability to vote directly for or against board members through proxy votes. Citizen-owners of the USPS do not have that right. A legal battle fought in the final days of the George H. W. Bush administration speaks to public lack of control over postal board members.[117] A federal court ruled that the president, acting on behalf of voters, does not have the power of removal over board members because removal power would violate the independence of the Postal Service. Academic inquiry suggests that the president's power to remove officials may be more important than the power of appointment.[118]

In early January 1993 President Bush sent letters to members of the board of governors threatening to remove them if they did not abandon their legal challenge to a two-cent discount for bar-coded, machine-processed first-class mail, which the Postal Rate Commission supported.[119] On January 7 Judge Louis Oberdorfer of the U.S. District Court in Washington temporarily barred the president from carrying out that threat.[120] The judge ruled that the Postal Service was an independent agency, outside the control of the executive. On January 8 President Bush defied the injunction and attempted to replace one member of the board.[121] On January 16 a federal court ruled that the president could not dismiss members of the board of governors.[122] As a result U.S. citizens apparently have no legal rights of removal over the members of the board of governors through any elected representative. The board, which is supposed to act in citizens' interests, is completely out of their control. That situation certainly compounds the agency problems in the Postal Service to a level beyond that in any private corporation. Private firm owners can directly vote board members off the board by proxy.

Thus, the creation of the board of governors achieved managerial autonomy only by placing the board completely out of control of the people who matter most: the citizen-owners of the Postal Service. In doing so, it worsened agency problems. Although the board has robust authority to overrule its regulator, it lacks accountability. In that sense the act failed to imitate the governance structure of a privately owned corporation.

Labor Relations

A key goal of the act was to reform the personnel system that Congress had managed directly since the Post Office's inception. Postal workers were loath to relinquish their hard-won influence over Congress, however, and resisted the creation of an independent personnel system. Through a two-part pay raise–collective bargaining arrangement at the time of the act, an agreement was reached between the federal government and the craft unions that gained organized labor's agreement. All federal employees would receive a 6 percent raise, retroactive to December 27, 1969, and postal employees would receive an additional 8 percent as part of the Reorganization Act.[123] Collective bargaining was mandated for wages, hours, working conditions, and grievances, as well as other matters normally subject to collective bargaining in the private sector.[124]

Consolidation of the craft unions substantially increased the political power of postal workers. The principal unions involved were the National Association of Letter Carriers, AFL-CIO (city letter carriers), the National Association of Post Office and General Services Maintenance Employees, AFL-CIO (maintenance employees), the National Federation of Post Office Motor Vehicle Employees, AFL-CIO (motor vehicle employees and postal clerks); the National Rural Letter Carriers Association (rural letter carriers); the American Postal Workers Union, AFL-CIO (postal clerks); and the National Post Office Mail Handlers, Watchmen, Messengers and Group Leaders Division of the Laborers' International Union of North America, AFL-CIO (mail handlers). Altogether they represented approximately 700,000 members.[125] A no-layoff policy applies to many employees, and unions do not have the right to strike.[126]

Although Congress has no direct oversight of wage setting, the act requires that wages paid to postal workers be comparable to those of their private sector counterparts: "It shall be the policy of the Postal Service to maintain compensation and benefits for all officers and employees on a standard of comparability to the compensation and benefits paid for comparable levels of work in the private sector of the economy."[127] The act, however, provided no mechanism to ensure that requirement. Many empirical studies confirm that the wage comparability standard has not been met. In two studies Sharon Smith found that postal workers were paid more than the comparable private sector wage.[128] Douglas Adie found that postal salaries were 40 percent higher than competitive rates.[129] Jeffrey Perloff and Michael Wachter similarly found that in 1978 postal salaries were 21.2 percent higher than for similar workers in the private sector.[130] Wachter and Perloff again found a postal wage premium of 21.3 percent when using 1988 data,[131] while Barry Hirsch, Michael Wachter, and James Gillula found a wage premium of 28 percent.[132] Postal workers apparently benefited through the act from their enhanced power and reduced congressional oversight. Analysis of data presented in chapter 4 confirms that conclusion.

Congressional Oversight

The executive branch's lack of control over the USPS naturally shifts focus to congressional oversight. Congress exercises oversight through several channels, but each provides only weak control over the USPS. The outcome is unsurprising because a key goal of the act was to reduce congressional involvement in its operations.

Some congressional oversight remains through appropriations for certain subsidized services, including public service subsidies (to meet service obligations in particular communities), transitional subsidies (for costs of the Post Office, such as unfunded workers' compensation and other liabilities), and "revenue forgone" appropriations (which allow reduced rates for nonprofit organizations, library materials, and mail for the blind). Since 1981 the subsidy for public service has been slight, and transitional subsidies have been gradually phased out.[133] The revenue forgone appropriation of $71 million in 1999 was only 0.11 percent of USPS operating revenues that year. Any "power of the purse" that Congress exercises over the USPS is minimal, as intended by the act.

The Senate has advice and consent authority over board and Postal Rate Commission appointments, and Congress can hold hearings to examine various aspects of postal operations.[134] The General Accounting Office is Congress's main auditor and program evaluator. Before the Postal Reorganization Act was passed, the GAO had statutory authority to prohibit the expenditures of Post Office funds when it concluded that such expenditures were unauthorized by law.[135] The act eliminated that power. The act also allowed the Postal Service to settle certain types of claims without going through the GAO. The GAO's power to stipulate postal accounting standards and principles was also eliminated.[136] The Postal Reorganization Act did provide for some periodic reporting from the GAO through the requirement that "the accounts and operations of the Postal Service shall be audited by the Comptroller General and reports thereon made to the Congress to the extent and at such times as he may determine."[137] Such reports, however, have no binding legal authority on the USPS.

The Postal Service is thus quite independent of Congress. Other scholars have noted the change. As Yale economist Sharon Oster states, "In sum, the Act replaced the overly-meddlesome, highly politicized oversight of the postal organization by Congress with oversight by a board which is under almost no control at all, coupled with sporadic Congressional inquiry when particular interests are threatened!"[138]

Summary

This chapter has provided an overview of the Postal Reorganization Act's main features. The act in effect transferred control of the Postal Service from Congress to the USPS itself. The resulting organization remained a government-owned monopoly but was quite independent of Congress. Although rates and costs were more closely linked through the act, the Postal Rate Commission was not given adequate authority to constrain either cross-subsidies or total costs. Postal workers were given more independence and more bargaining power but were not subjected to the necessary regulatory or market oversight.

Although the act successfully reduced direct political control over the USPS, the retention of government ownership and legally enforced monopoly disallowed market forces from constraining the Postal Service. The Postal Service now seems accountable to no one, neither citizen-taxpayers nor shareholders. Numerous commentators have recognized the weakness of the act. Sidak and Spulber state: "Unfortunately, the current forms of public control of the Postal Service are ineffectual. In essence, the Postal Service is an unregulated monopolist that is constrained only in the sense that it is expedient for the enterprise not to show a profit."[139] Similarly, in 1981, consumer advocate Ralph Nader noted that

> the new 20-cent first-class stamp represents not only runaway postal costs but also the unchecked power of the Postal Service. The new rate came about because the mail system's Board of Governors

deliberately overrode the Postal Rate Commission (P.R.C.), which, on three separate occasions, had found the latest increase unnecessary. We can only conclude that the Postal Service is no longer accountable to anyone—not to the P.R.C., not to the President, not to Congress and certainly not to the American people.[140]

4

The Effects of the Postal
Reorganization Act

In this chapter I assess the impact of the institutional changes introduced
by the Postal Reorganization Act on key variables by examining data
across time. Those variables include postal rates, relative salaries, productivity and efficiency, net income, taxpayer's equity, and government
appropriations. I briefly review previous research on the act, describe the
data to be used, and present summary statistics. I break the sample down
into pre- and postact years, and report t-statistics for the difference. I
then graphically display the data and describe an empirical technique
that allows statistical assessment of the act's effects. The exposition is
more technical in this chapter; some readers may wish to move directly
to chapter 5.

Previous Research on the Act

A surprisingly limited amount of empirical work examines the act's
effects. Although Sam Peltzman's essay (1989) did not explicitly focus on
the act's effects, he examined pertinent data.[1] He compared average
growth rates in productivity, relative wages, unit costs, and prices before
the act (1960–1970) and after the act (1970–1983). He concluded that
productivity increased faster after the act (from 0.1 percent to 3.3 percent per year) and that relative wages grew faster after the act (from 1.1
percent to 2.0 percent per year) but that productivity increased by more
than wages increased. Therefore unit costs, which had been increasing,
declined after the act (from 1.2 percent to -1.0 percent per year).
Peltzman found that postal customers, however, did not benefit from

productivity increases or cost decreases. Real prices increased faster after the act (from 0.7 percent to 1.1 percent per year). He concluded that postal workers benefited from the act, as did Congress, which, due to declining unit costs, faced a lower deficit than before the act. Paul MacAvoy and George McIssac noted that postal rates increased faster than the rate of inflation after the act.[2]

Donald Ewing and Roger Salaman conducted a detailed study of the Postal Service from 1945 to 1975.[3] They concluded that productivity improved over that period, postal salaries increased, but cost efficiency decreased. The brief time after the act's passage, however, did not allow them to focus rigorously on its effects.

Data Description and Means Tests

I used the *Annual Report of the Postmaster General,* later termed the *U.S. Postal Service Annual Report,* as the central data source. Additional data sources are described in appendix A. Data were available for most variables for 1930 through 1997. Data on prices were available from 1945 only. Data on postal salaries were available for 1930 to 1996. Data on express mail prices are available from the creation of that mail class in 1978 to 1997.

Table 4-1 provides variable names, definitions, and summary statistics for all years, for pre-act and postact years, and for the changes. All monetary values are expressed in constant 1987 dollars. Comparisons of mean values pre- and postact were conducted with small-sample *t*-statistics, which appear in brackets.

The variables are divided into four groups. The first group, rates, measures the overall real price of mail (PRICE), real prices for each of the traditional major mail classes (PRICE1 through PRICE4), real express mail prices (PRICEXP), and the ratio of first-class to express mail prices (RATIO).[4] All variables on rates display statistically significant differences pre- and postact, with real fourth-class mail prices notably showing the only decrease.

The second variable group, salaries, provides data on annual postal salaries (SAL) and five employment categories (government, manufacturing, services, communications, and utilities). With the exception of manufacturing, the categories were chosen to reflect alternative perceptions of the postal function. Manufacturing broadens the basis for comparison. Annual postal salaries are divided by the average annual salaries in each of those groups to provide relative salary measures, named RELG, RELM, RELS, RELC, and RELU, respectively. Two relative salary measures display increases, while three show declines.

The third variable group, productivity and efficiency, provides two measures of the size of the postal work force: the total number of postal employees (WORKER1) and the number of career employees (WORKER2).[5] Those two variables are used to create four measures of labor productivity: postal sales per worker (SALESPER1, SALESPER2) and pieces delivered per worker (PCEPER1, PCEPER2) for each worker category. Total factor productivity (TFP) is also included. All measures show statistically significant increases after the act. As a measure of efficiency, the pieces of mail delivered per 1987 dollar (PCPDOL) is also reported. Cost efficiency shows no change from pre- to postact years.

The final variable group, taxpayers, reports summary statistics and means tests for real postal net income (INCOME), taxpayer's equity (EQUITY), and annual government appropriations (APPR). Although net income was significantly higher after the act, both equity and government appropriations were lower. The latter change, however, is not statistically significant.

Empirical Technique

Using time-series tests for structural breaks, I assess the effects of postal reorganization in addition to examining data graphically. One approach is to use classical regression analysis and include a dummy variable for pre- and postact years. That approach leads to errors in inference if the series is nonstationary because the assumptions of the classical regression model are not fulfilled.[6] The problem does not disappear in large samples. Nonstationarity can be detected through the use of unit-root tests.[7] Using a modified version of Perron's 1989 test for structural change, for any variable y I estimate the equation

Table 4-1 Variables, Descriptive Statistics, and Means Tests

Variable	Description	All Years	1945–1970	1971–1997	Change
Rates					
PRICE	The real price of all mail, defined as revenues from mail divided by total pieces	0.198 (0.025)	0.179 (0.02)	0.216 (0.011)	0.037 [8.351][a]
PRICE1	The real price of first-class mail, defined as revenue from first class divided by its volume	0.207 (0.042)	0.170 (0.024)	0.243 (0.016)	0.073 [12.969][a]
PRICE2	The real price of second-class mail, defined as revenue from second class divided by its volume	0.075 (0.042)	0.041 (0.006)	0.107 (0.035)	0.066 [9.744][a]
PRICE3	The real price of third-class mail, defined as revenue from third class divided by its volume	0.104 (0.02)	0.092 (0.02)	0.116 (0.01)	0.024 [5.59][a]
PRICE4	The real price of fourth-class mail, defined as revenue from fourth class divided by its volume	1.767 (0.421)	1.984 (0.402)	1.557 (0.326)	-0.427 [-4.237][a]
PRICEXP	The real price of express mail, defined as revenue from express mail divided by its volume (1978–1997)	11.884 (2.640)	—	—	—
RATIO	The ratio of first-class to express mail prices	0.022 (0.004)	—	—	—

Salaries			1930–1970	1971–1996	
SAL	The real annual salaries of postal workers, defined as salary expenditures divided by total employees (1930–1996)	21,049 (5,790)	16,914 (3,088)	27,571 (981)	10,657 [20.53][a]
GOVS	The real annual average salary of government workers	18,756 (4,858)	15,513 (3,205)	23,870 (1,190)	8,357 [15.13][a]
MFGS	The real annual average salary of workers in manufacturing	20,378 (5,348)	17,039 (4,109)	25,644 (1,168)	8,605 [12.63][a]
SERS	The real annual average salary of workers in services	14,783 (4,746)	11,494 (2,692)	19,970 (1,460)	8,476 [16.66][a]
COMS	The real annual average salary of workers in communications	22,515 (8,197)	16,601 (3,733)	31,840 (2,700)	15,239 [19.35][a]
UTILS	The real annual average salary of workers in utilities	24,466 (7,652)	19,265 (4,417)	32,668 (3,005)	13,403 [14.77][a]
RELG	Postal relative to government salaries, defined as SAL divided by GOVS	1.122 (0.090)	1.098 (0.090)	1.158 (0.0788)	0.06 [2.872][a]

(table continues on next page)

51

Table 4-1 (continued) Variables, Descriptive Statistics, and Means Tests

Variable Name	Description	All Years	1930–1970	1971–1996	Change
RELM	Postal relative to manufacturing salaries, defined as SAL divided by MFGS	1.041 (0.138)	1.019 (0.167)	1.077 (0.0543)	0.058 [2.059]a
RELS	Postal relative to service salaries, defined as SAL divided by SERS	1.455 (0.168)	1.498 (0.186)	1.387 (0.108)	-0.111 [-2.763]a
RELC	Postal relative to communications salaries, defined as SAL divided by COMS	0.968 (0.112)	1.030 (0.090)	0.871 (0.0631)	-0.159 [-8.492]a
RELU	Postal relative to government salaries, defined as SAL divided by UTILS	0.874 (0.082)	0.889 (0.082)	0.85 (0.0764)	-0.039 [-1.980]
Productivity and Efficiency			1930–1970	1971–1997	
WORKER1	The total number of postal employees, in thousands	592.12 (175.13)	483.68 (128.96)	756.78 (82.146)	273.10 [9.63]a
WORKER2	The number of career postal employees only, in thousands	466.78 (173.94)	349.44 (92.63)	644.96 (100.42)	295.52 [12.31]a
SALESPER1	Real sales per worker, defined as revenues divided by WORKER1	27,145 (10,468)	19,681 (3,242.1)	38,480 (6,704.8)	18,799 [15.35]a
SALESPER2	Real sales per worker, defined as revenues divided by WORKER2	34,315 (10,363)	27,139 (4,168.8)	45,212 (6,743.2)	18,073 [13.56]a

Variable Name	Description	All Years	1930–1970	1971–1997	Change
PCEPER1	Labor productivity, defined as total number of pieces divided by WORKER1	124.91 (45.35)	93.84 (17.31)	172.10 (31.692)	78.26 [13.04]a
PCEPER2	Labor productivity, defined as total number of pieces divided by WORKER2	158.37 (44.14)	129.77 (24.10)	201.80 (29.661)	72.03 [10.88]a
TFP	Total factor productivity, as calculated by Laurits R. Christensen Associates (1963–1992)	1.023 (0.033)	0.979 (0.007)	1.039 (0.022)	0.060 [11.38]a
PCPDOL	Pieces of mail delivered per 1987 dollar, defined as total pieces delivered divided by annual real expenditures	4.129 (0.490)	4.096 (0.493)	4.180 (0.491)	0.084 [0.689]
Taxpayers					
INCOME	The annual real net income of the Postal Service, in millions	-1,156.4 (1,321.4)	-1,707.5 (1,261.5)	-319.57 (919.44)	1,387.93 [4.85]a
EQUITY	The annual real level of taxpayer's equity, in millions (1962–1997)	369.37 (2,503.3)	3,042.6 (582.86)	-521.7 (2,243.5)	-3,564.3 [-7.53]a
APPR	Annual real government appropriations, in millions	1,675.6 (1,365.0)	1,734.0 (1,274.7)	1,587.1 (1,512.6)	-146.9 [-0.42]

NOTE: Standard deviations are in parentheses. The t-statistics for "change" are in brackets.
a. A t-statistic significant at the 5 percent level. Monetary values are expressed in 1987 dollars. Data are available for the years noted in column headings. See appendix A for data sources.

$$y_t = \alpha_o + \alpha_1 y_{t-1} + \alpha_2 t + \mu D_A + \sum_{i=1}^{k} \beta_i \Delta y_{t-1} + \varepsilon_i$$

(4-1)

where the "act dummy" D_A equals 1 for all t beginning in 1971 and is zero otherwise. Here i runs from 1 to k, where k is the number of lags. Lag length k was chosen by starting with an excessively large number of lags and reducing that number until the Akaike information criterion (AIC) was minimized.[8]

To test the unit-root hypothesis, the t-statistic for the difference α_1 is from unity was compared with the critical value reported by Perron.[9] If the t-statistic is greater than that critical value, then the null hypothesis of a unit root can be rejected, and inferences can be made with confidence.[10] When the t-statistic was less than that critical value, I imposed a unit root by taking differences of the series and reporting results including an intercept term and act dummy.[11] The coefficient μ provides an estimate of the act's effects. The long-run impact of the act on y_t is given by $\frac{\mu}{1-\alpha_1}$.[12]

The procedure is appropriate for testing reorganization's effects for several reasons. First, it is appropriate where changes in levels and changes in rates of growth can be modeled as exogenous, as with postal reorganization.[13] Second, the date of reorganization is known, and we wish to assess its effects. By utilizing dummy variables, the model assumes a single break at a known point in time.[14] Third, the approach provides a single test that can at once distinguish between a unit-root process and a trend-stationary series that has a single break.[15] The procedure is applied to key variables presented in table 4-1, and results are described in variable groups below, along with graphical evidence.

Postal Rates

Figures 4-1 through 4-7 display graphical evidence on real mail prices. Figure 4-1 displays the real price of all mail in 1987 dollars. It suggests that the upward trend in real mail prices observed before the act continued

Figure 4-1 Real Mail Prices (PRICE), 1945–1997

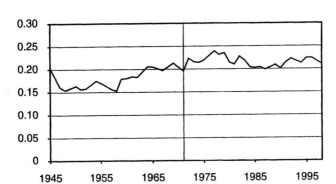

after the act was passed but then leveled off by the late 1970s. The real price has drifted between 20 and 25 cents per piece since then. The mean of the series is clearly higher after the act, as suggested in table 4-1. Table 4-2 presents the results of time-series tests on this variable. The series is stationary, and the act dummy indicates a strong, positive effect of the act on total real mail prices. The estimated long-run effect of the act was to increase total prices by about 3.2 percent. The result is unsurprising because one goal of the act was to place more cost of mail service onto users of mail rather than taxpayers.

Figure 4-2 displays the real price of first-class mail, the largest and most monopolized class. The price suggests a greater postact increase than total mail prices, with a particularly large increase soon after the act. The real unit price of first-class mail at implementation (in 1987 dollars) was 18.89 cents. It reached a high of 26.37 cents in 1982, an increase of 40 percent. It subsequently fell to 24.66 cents in 1997. First-class prices have leveled off in recent years. It is difficult to assess the cause of the recent leveling. It may be the result of the increasing availability of substitutes for letters, such as lower-cost long-distance phone service, facsimile machines, and electronic mail.[16]

Results in table 4-2 indicate that the series is stationary and suggest that the act had a strong, positive effect on first-class mail prices on top of an already strong, positive time trend. That finding is quite consistent with anecdotal evidence indicating that first-class rates were too high

Figure 4-2   Price of First-Class Mail (PRICE1), 1945–1997

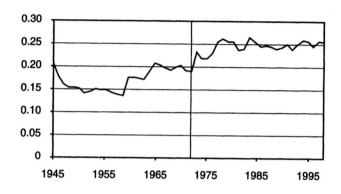

before the act but were exacerbated by the act through the Postal Rate Commission's lack of power to control increasing cross-subsidies. Table 4-2 indicates that the long-term effect of the act was to increase first-class rates by about 3 percent, while table 4-1 shows that first-class rates were 7.3 cents, or 43 percent, higher after the act. That finding may be due to the fact that first-class rates were rising independently of the act (see the time-trend column of table 4-2), as some commentators have suggested.

Figure 4-3 displays the real price of second-class mail, now called periodicals, which includes newspapers, magazines, and other periodicals. Second-class mail is a relatively small mail class, currently accounting for about 3.5 percent of total mail revenues. Figure 4-3 shows a particularly large increase through the late 1970s, with a slower but steady increase thereafter. Time-series tests indicate that this variable is nonstationary; inferences using Perron's technique are not reliable. I thus differenced the series. Results are reported in table 4-2 in the row entitled DIFF PRICE2. The difference indicates that the act had a strong, positive effect on second-class mail users. Table 4-1 shows that the mean was about 6.6 cents higher after the act.

Figure 4-4 displays the real price of third-class mail, now called standard mail A. Third-class mail is mostly printed advertising, solicitation, and promotional material. Businesses are the primary senders of third-class mail, which currently accounts for about 24 percent of total revenues from mail. Figure 4-4 suggests that real third-class rates continued a slight

Table 4-2 Intervention Estimates of the Effect of Postal Reorganization on Mail Prices

Variable	Sample Size	Number of Lags	Constant	Act Dummy	Time Trend	Pre-Act Mean	Long-Run Effect
PRICE	45	7	-0.196 (-0.762)	0.0133 (3.247)a	0.0001 (1.031)	0.179 [0.02]	0.032
PRICE1	45	7	-1.850 (-4.028)a	0.016 (3.262)a	0.001 (4.128)a	0.168 [0.023]	0.029
PRICE2	51	1	-0.400 (-1.380)	0.0002 (0.054)	0.0002 (1.386)	0.041 [0.006]	0.002
DIFF PRICE2	52	0	0.0005 (0.381)	0.003 (1.788)a	—	—	—
PRICE3	43	9	0.060 (0.357)	0.008 (2.579)a	-0.00002 (-0.216)	0.092 [0.02]	0.030
PRICE4	51	1	2.897 (0.947)	-0.0006 (-0.012)	-0.0014 (-0.898)	2.003 [0.398]	-0.008
DIFF PRICE4	52	0	0.030 (1.204)	-0.069 (-1.981)a	—	—	—

NOTE: Data are from 1946 through 1997. Standard deviations for means are in brackets. The t-statistics are in parentheses. First-differences are reported where a series is nonstationary after the appropriate number of lags is taken.
a. Significant at the .05 level, one-tailed test for act dummy, two-tailed test for constant and time trend.

Figure 4-3 Price of Second-Class Mail (PRICE2), 1945–1997

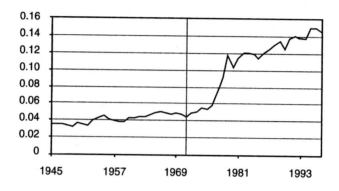

Figure 4-4 Price of Third-Class Mail (PRICE3), 1945–1997

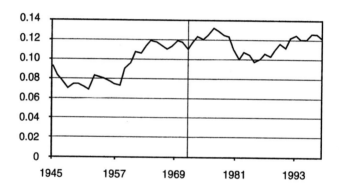

upward pre-act trend until the late 1970s and then declined into the 1980s before resuming that trend. Average third-class rates were 11.08 cents in 1971 and increased to 13.22 cents in 1976 before declining. Time-series estimates in table 4-2 for third-class mail (PRICE3) indicate that the act had a positive and significant effect on third-class mail prices.

Figure 4-5 displays the real price of fourth-class-mail, now called standard mail B. Fourth-class mail contains four subclasses: parcel post, bound printed matter, special rate, and library rate. In general, fourth-class mail tends to contain tangible objects (for example, merchandise, household items) rather than correspondence.[17] Private firms, such as United Parcel Service, compete intensively for fourth-class package business. Fourth-class mail is unusual in that it displays a sustained downward trend

Figure 4-5 Price of Fourth-Class Mail (PRICE4), 1945–1997

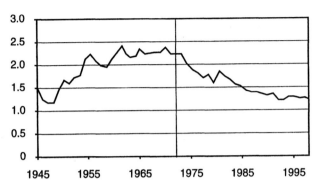

in price since the act. The average real price per piece was $2.28 in 1971 and reached a low of $1.21 in 1996, a decrease of 47 percent. That trend contrasts sharply with the mail classes discussed above. Since the fourth-class time series was not stationary, I differenced the series and report results in the row entitled DIFF PRICE4 in table 4-2. The test indicates a strong, negative effect of the act on real fourth-class mail rates and is consistent with table 4-1, which shows a decrease of 42.7 cents since the act.

The final class of mail examined is express mail, as displayed in figure 4-6. Express mail is extremely urgent material. Express mail currently accounts for about 1.6 percent of total mail revenues and faces competition from several overnight delivery companies, including Federal Express, United Parcel Service's overnight service, and DHL. The act's effect on express mail cannot be examined explicitly because it was created after the act's implementation, in October 1977. Because the mail class faces intense competition, it is useful to examine its price behavior over time. Data for express mail prices from 1978 to the present show a pattern remarkably similar to the postact behavior of fourth-class mail. There was a decrease soon after inception, followed by a leveling off of prices.

Figure 4-7 displays the ratio of first-class to express mail prices. If the act created a relatively weak regulatory structure through the powers granted to the Postal Rate Commission and the lack of tradable ownership shares, then this would manifest itself through an inability to restrain revenue maximizing cross-subsidy from monopolistic to

Figure 4-6   Price of Express Mail (PRICEXP), 1978–1997

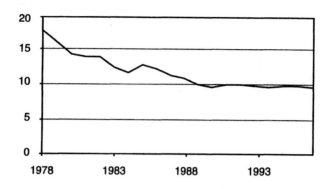

Figure 4-7   Ratio of First-Class to Express Mail Prices (RATIO), 1978–1997

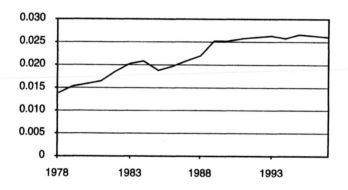

competitive mail classes.[18] Congress, while clearly subject to political pressure before the act, was able to set rates directly and constrain such cross-subsidy if it wished. The hypothesis of a weak regulator predicts that first-class relative to express mail rates will increase after the act.

Figure 4-7, displaying the ratio of first-class to express mail prices (RATIO), provides a test of that hypothesis. That ratio shows a significant increase of about 70 percent since 1978. Express mail is highly competitive because it competes with Federal Express, UPS Overnight, and other services. As noted, it is not possible to examine the act's effect on this ratio. The strong positive trend since 1977 evident in figure 4-7, however, is consistent with increasing cross-subsidy to this mail class.

Postal Salaries

Figures 4-8 through 4-12 display the effects of the act on postal relative to other salaries. Included for comparison are government workers, manufacturing workers, service workers, communications workers, and utility workers. With the exception of salaries relative to communications workers in figure 4-11, the series displays remarkably similar patterns. Postal salaries were relatively high during the depression, fell throughout World War II, and were constant throughout the postwar period. Each measure suggests that relative postal salaries received a significant boost after the act (particularly relative to other government workers), typically returning relative salaries to late depression-era levels. All series display a downturn in relative salaries in the mid-1980s, when increases in first-class and total mail rates also slowed. Because salary and benefits account for about 80 percent of the Postal Service's total costs, and the agency is required to break even, any slowdown in revenue will quickly affect wage increases. The observed slowdown in salaries may also be explained by the increasing availability and use of substitutes for letter delivery.[19]

Table 4-3 reports the results of time-series estimates on all relative wage variables. All variables are stationary except for postal relative to manufacturing salaries. With the exception of postal relative to salaries in communications, all series display a significant and positive effect of the act. The strongest effects are for salaries relative to government, service, and utility workers. Long-run effects suggest that the act also had an economically significant impact on relative salaries compared to the pre-act mean. The act increased the ratio of postal workers' salaries to government and service workers by more than 10 percent, by more than 9 percent relative to workers in utilities, and by more than 14 percent relative to service workers. The evidence is consistent with postal workers extracting more economic rent in the form of salaries after reorganization.[20]

Estimates are also consistent with those of other researchers. Ewing and Salaman, for example, summarize their findings: "A postal career has traditionally been viewed as being secure, but relatively low paying.

Figure 4-8 Postal Salaries Relative to Government Workers
(RELG), 1930–1996

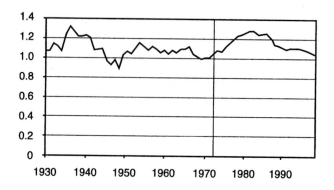

Figure 4-9 Postal Salaries Relative to Manufacturing Workers
(RELM), 1930–1996

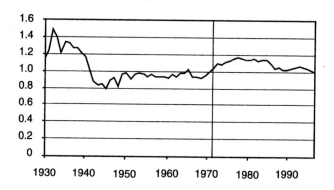

Figure 4-10 Postal Salaries Relative to Service Workers (RELS),
1930–1996

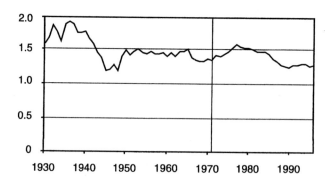

Figure 4-11 Postal Salaries Relative to Communications Workers (RELC), 1930–1996

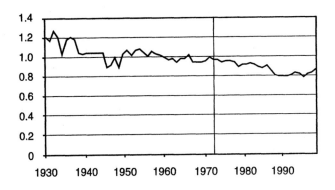

Figure 4-12 Postal Salaries Relative to Utility Workers (RELU), 1930–1996

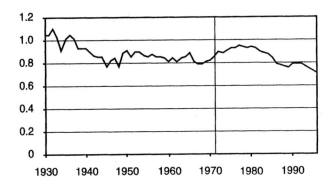

However, not only has the Postal Reorganization Act with its provision for collective bargaining brought about definitely higher postal salaries, but postal salaries have increased at a higher rate than has the salary of the average American worker."[21]

Productivity and Efficiency

One key goal of the act was to improve the efficiency of postal operations through improved management techniques. Figures 4-13 through 4-18 present several variables measuring productivity and efficiency.

Table 4-3 Intervention Estimates of the Effect of Postal Reorganization on Relative Salaries

Variable	Sample Size	Number of Lags	Constant	Act Dummy	Time Trend	Pre-Act Mean	Long-Run Effect
RELG	58	8	1.260 (1.455)	0.032 (1.926)a	-0.0005 (-1.094)	1.098 [0.43]	0.103
RELM	61	5	1.029 (1.084)	0.026 (1.421)b	-0.0005 (-0.974)	1.019 [1.083]	0.197
DIFF RELM	67	0	-24.369 (-1.275)	24.369 (0.794)	—	—	—
RELS	59	7	4.269 (2.725)a	0.040 (1.783)a	-0.002 (-2.574)a	1.498 [0.508]	0.144
RELC	57	9	6.575 (5.929)a	0.010 (0.878)	-0.003 (-5.683)a	1.030 [0.823]	0.016
RELU	57	9	3.584 (3.841)a	0.041 (3.070)a	-0.0016 (-3.647)a	0.889 [0.958]	0.094

NOTE: Data are from 1930 through 1996. Standard deviations for means are in brackets. The t-statistics are in parentheses. Where a series is nonstationary after the appropriate number of lags is taken, estimates for first differences are also reported. Nonstationarity can be rejected for the RELM series at the 10 percent level.
a. Significant at the .05 level, one-tailed test for act dummy, two-tailed test for constant and time trend.
b. Significant at the .10 level.

**Figure 4-13 Real Sales per Postal Worker (SALESPER1),
1930–1997**

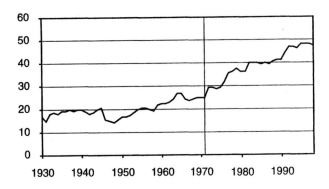

Figure 4-13 displays real sales per postal worker. With the exception of a slowdown in the mid-1980s, that measure of productivity has improved steadily since the act. It rose from $24,643 of real sales per worker in 1971 to $47,977 in 1997, an increase of 95 percent. The conclusion is supported by time-series tests reported in table 4-4, which in a differenced series indicate that SALESPER1 increased significantly as a result of the act. That result is also consistent with means tests in table 4-1, which indicate an increase of $19,000 in the variable after the act.

Figure 4-14, dividing sales by career employees only, displays a greater reduction in the mid-1980s but with a larger increase in the 1990s. That measure rose from $32,903 of real sales per worker in 1971 to $56,977 in 1997. Tests using differences in the series, however, indicate that the act's effect on the series was not significantly different from zero.

Figures 4-15 and 4-16, measuring labor productivity as pieces delivered per worker (PCEPER1 and PCEPER2), display similar patterns to figures 4-13 and 4-14. While increasing slowly since the early depression years, labor productivity appears to have risen more rapidly since the act. That trend is particularly striking in figure 4-16, which displays pieces delivered per career worker. Pieces per career worker increased almost 57 percent in the twenty-six years from 1971 to 1997 but only a little more than 46 percent in the forty-one years from 1930 through 1971. Time-series tests on those variables are somewhat less conclusive,

Table 4-4 Intervention Estimates of the Effect of Postal Reorganization on Productivity and Efficiency

Variable	Sample Size	Number of Lags	Constant	Act Dummy	Time Trend	Pre-Act Mean	Long-Run Effect
SALESPER1	63	4	-27,792 (-0.097)	8.709 (0.136)	14.254 (0.093)	19,681 [3,242.1]	123.20
DIFF SALESPER1	67	0	-735.87 (-0.951)	6.328 (1.599)[a]	—	—	—
SALESPER2	67	0	304,900 (0.856)	114.21 (1.378)	-162.84 (-0.861)	27,139 [4,167.8]	617.15
DIFF SALESPER2	67	0	-622.75 (-0.543)	5.927 (1.010)	—	—	—
PCEPER1	58	9	-1,156.7 (-1.138)	-0.191 (-0.919)	0.611 (1.134)	93.835 [17.307]	-3.164

DIFF PCEPER1	67	0	-2.900 (-1.312)	0.0256 (2.262)[b]	—	—	—
PCEPER2	67	0	-2,512.3 (-2.326)[b]	-0.388 (-1.619)[a]	1.332 (2.322)[b]	129.77 [24.10]	2.207
DIFF PCEPER2	67	0	-2.207 (-0.624)	0.023 (1.285)	—	—	—
TFP	28	1	-5.257 (-0.328)	-0.0006 (-0.167)	0.003 (0.347)	0.979 [0.007]	-0.001
PCPDOL	64	3	-54.926 (1.142)	-0.012 (-1.140)	0.026 (1.153)	4.096 [0.493]	0.069

NOTE: Data are from 1930 through 1997. Standard deviations for means are in brackets. The *t*-statistics are in parentheses.
a. Significant at the .10 level; one-tailed test for act dummy, two-tailed test for constant and time trend.
b. Significant at the .05 level; one-tailed test for act dummy, two-tailed test for constant and time trend.

Figure 4-14 Real Sales per Career Postal Worker (SALESPER2), 1930–1997

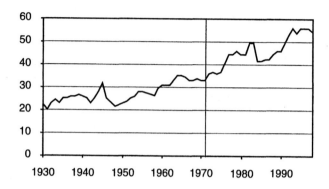

Figure 4-15 Labor Productivity by Pieces per Postal Worker (PCEPER1), 1930–1997

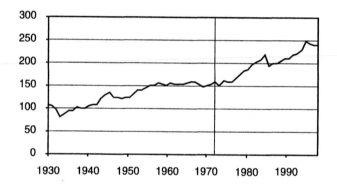

Figure 4-16 Labor Productivity by Pieces per Career Worker (PCEPER2), 1930–1997

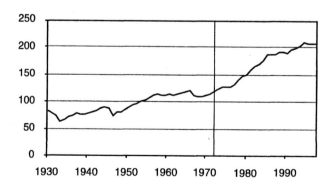

however. They indicate that the differenced pieces-per-postal-worker series was improved by the act, while the pieces-per-career-postal worker measure was actually reduced, but on top of a positive time-trend.

The final measure of productivity is total factor productivity, which considers the contribution of all inputs to output[22] and is displayed in figure 4-17. Data show a rapid increase in total factor productivity immediately after the act, with slower but continued improvement since the 1980s. Total factor productivity, though stationary, shows no effect of the act. The result may be due to the small number of pre-act observations on TFP, however. Figure 4-17 is consistent with other figures showing postact productivity improvement, and the weight of the evidence suggests that the act did improve postal productivity.

The final variable examined in this group, PCPDOL, or the number of pieces delivered per real dollar spent by the Postal Service, does not measure productivity but rather cost efficiency. PCPDOL is displayed in figure 4-18. Clearly the act did not initially affect a negative trend in that variable. Although cost-efficiency improved from 3.60 pieces delivered per real dollar spent in 1971 to about 4.5 pieces per real dollar in the mid-1980s, it nevertheless only reached the level enjoyed in the mid-1950s, and has never reattained the high level of 5 pieces delivered per dollar spent in 1945. Time-series tests in table 4-4 support those inferences. The stationary series indicates that the act had no appreciable effect on the cost efficiency of the Postal Service. Where have gains in productivity gone? One possibility is that they were captured by politically effective groups, such as labor, through higher wages.

Taxpayers

Figures 4-19 through 4-21 display net income, government appropriations, and equity. An important goal of the act was to make the Postal Service financially self-sufficient. It was to break even on an annual basis and therefore reduce its charge on the Treasury, that is, on the taxpayer. Figure 4-19 shows that the USPS has essentially achieved that goal. Net income (INCOME) hovered around minus $3 billion before the act but, with the exception of some early losses, approximately broke even after

Figure 4-17   Total Factor Productivity, 1963–1992

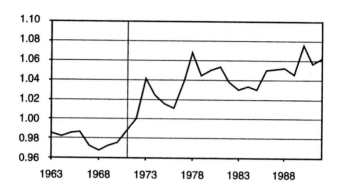

Figure 4-18   Cost-Efficiency by Pieces Delivered per 1987 Dollar (PCPDOL), 1930–1997

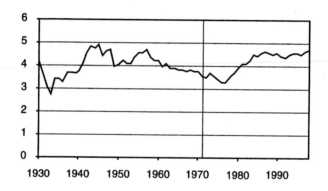

the act. That situation is consistent with means tests on net income but not with time-series tests reported in table 4-5, which indicate that the act actually reduced net income on top of a positive time trend. That effect may reflect the Postal Service's early financial difficulties rather than a long-term trend.

Figure 4-20 displays annual government appropriations. As is clear from the figure, while a substantial one-time outlay occurred at the time of the act, annual appropriations have decreased to almost zero.[23] That finding is consistent with figure 4-19 and with the USPS breaking even after the act. Graphical evidence clearly indicates that the act assisted in

Figure 4-19 USPS Net Income (INCOME), 1950–1997

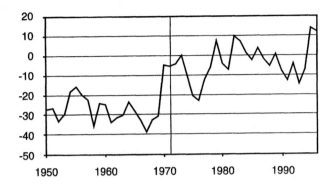

Figure 4-20 Government Appropriations (APPR), 1930–1995 (millions of 1987 dollars)

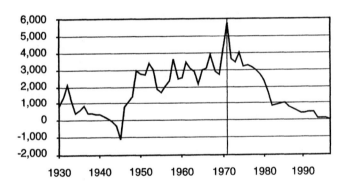

reducing the charge on the Treasury, while both means-tests and time-series estimates show no effect, probably because of the extreme variance of the series. If 1971 is removed from the data set, however, a negative and significant effect of the act on government appropriations occurs, but the series is not stationary.

Figure 4-21, displaying taxpayer's equity, is consistent with figure 4-19.[24] When net income is negative, taxpayer's equity declines, and vice versa. The initial losses of the USPS in the early 1970s caused taxpayer equity to decline to approximately zero, and equity has never regained its previous levels. In real 1987 dollars, equity went from a high of more

Table 4-5 Intervention Estimates of the Effect of Postal Reorganization on Taxpayers

Variable	Sample Size	Number of Lags	Constant	Act Dummy	Time Trend	Pre-Act Mean	Long-Run Effect
INCOME	58	9	1,530,700 (-6.972)a	-332.28 (-6.938)a	810.92 (6.969)a	-1,707.5 [1,261.5]	-495.88
APPR	64	3	160,890 (1.311)	36.735 (1.329)b	-85.325 (-1.310)	667.89 [1,3014]	234.92
DIFF APPR	67	0	277.71 (0.779)	-1.518 (-0.832)	—	—	—
EQUITY	35	0	896,600 (0.994)	197.55 (0.935)	-475.59 (-0.991)	3,042.6 [582.86]	1,254.37
DIFF EQUITY	35	0	-844.60 (-0.565)	3.194 (0.489)	—	—	—

NOTE: Standard deviations for means are in brackets. The t-statistics are in parentheses.
a. Significant at the .05 level, one-tailed test for act dummy, two-tailed test for constant and time trend.
b. Significant at the .10 level, one-tailed test for act dummy, two-tailed test for constant and time trend.

Figure 4-21   Taxpayer's Equity, 1962–1997
(millions of 1987 dollars)

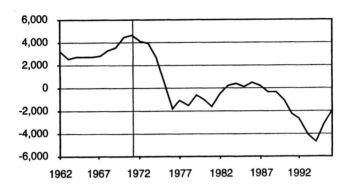

than $4.5 billion in 1971 to a low of less than negative $4 billion in 1993. That trend is consistent with means tests, which show a drop in equity of more than $3.5 billion after the act, but not with time-series tests, which indicate no change. Figure 4-21 suggests that the act has not prevented the Postal Service from depleting substantial amounts of taxpayer's equity. Given that no well-defined, transferable claims to the residual cash flow of the Postal Service exist, that conclusion is unsurprising.

Summary

This chapter presents evidence suggesting that the Postal Reorganization Act achieved the goals set forth by the Kappel commission in several critical ways. As suggested by figure 4-1, it succeeded in placing more of the total cost of mail onto mail users, rather than taxpayers. That conclusion is supported by figure 4-19, which indicates that the Postal Service has come much closer to breaking even after the act, and by figure 4-20, which displays a declining annual charge on the Treasury. Both results were important goals of the Kappel commission. As suggested by several measures, the act succeeded in improving postal productivity. Sales per employee, pieces per employee, and total factor productivity all display postact improvement. Moreover, there can be little doubt that the act made the Postal Service more independent of Congress.

But the act also failed in important ways. First, figure 4-7 suggests that the act increased the cross-subsidy from monopolized to competitive mail classes. Such cross-subsidies caused a great deal of concern at the time of the act's passage, but the act does not appear to have eliminated them. Second, both previous studies and the estimates reported here imply that postal wages have exceeded the comparability standard since the act and were probably increased by it. The analysis in chapter 3 indicates that the act provided insufficient institutional structures to achieve the comparability goal. Third, the productivity gains discussed do not appear to have been passed along to consumers. Figure 4-18 indicates that more pieces of mail were delivered per real dollar spent in 1944 than are delivered today. Given the massive productivity improvements in other communications industries over the past decades, that conclusion is striking. Fourth, the act failed to create institutional structures capable of protecting taxpayers' equity. Figure 4-21 indicates that significant amounts of taxpayers' equity have been depleted since the act's implementation. Whether the act can be considered a complete success depends inevitably on how one weighs those individual successes and failures. Regardless of the act's general effect, further postal reform is necessary, as discussed in chapter 5.

5

A Case for Postal Reform

Numerous arguments, usually focusing on the benefits of enhanced competition or private ownership, have been marshaled in support of postal reform. Those arguments include improved incentives for cost-minimization, better allocative efficiency, and better choice of firm size, as well as stronger incentives to innovate. Robert Hahn and John Hird, writing in 1991, estimated the annual cost of the delivery monopoly at $4–12 billion.[1] Thomas Lenard estimated the cost of just the third-class monopoly at around $1 billion in 1992.[2] Those costs were due to both allocative inefficiency—reduced output due to monopoly—and non–cost-minimizing behavior.

Rather than recounting all previous theories and evidence supporting reform in detail, I present three arguments for postal reform that are timely but relatively underappreciated. I first discuss the effects of transferable ownership shares, or residual claims, on the mechanisms available for controlling agency costs within the modern corporation. My analysis indicates that managers are likely to be more intensively monitored and to behave more efficiently in firms with transferable, rather than monopolized, ownership shares. I then review statistical evidence on the success of institutional reform of other network industries in the United States. Successful deregulation of other industries with structures similar to that of postal services suggests similar gains through postal reform. Third, I discuss how technological change is further weakening the two main arguments for government-enforced monopoly and government ownership of postal services: universal service and natural monopoly.

75

Transferable Ownership Shares and Agency Costs

Agency costs arise in any organization in which a firm's owners are a distinct group from its managers. Firm owners—for example, the stockholders in a corporation—would like managers to operate the firm as efficiently as possible, but managers often have other objectives, including higher salaries, more leisure time, more perks, and more job security. Agency costs include the costs of trying to align the incentives of a firm's managers with its owners', as well as the inevitable loss of firm value because those incentives will never be perfectly aligned without incurring infinite incentive-alignment costs.

Even since Adolph Berle and Gardiner Means pointed out the costs associated with this "separation of ownership and control,"[3] researchers have developed an appreciation for how the property rights arrangements defining the firm are crucial for the creation of solutions to the agency problem. A substantial body of literature in financial economics—broadly referred to as the corporate governance literature—presents studies of institutions that have evolved spontaneously to ameliorate the agency problem. Although that literature is too large to review here in its entirety, this section draws on it to compare two types of property rights structures and their implications for control of agency costs: the government-owned corporation and the privately owned, but public traded, corporation. The Postal Service is a government-owned entity. However, absent government intervention, it would likely be a privately owned corporation, as the Kappel commission envisioned.

Property Rights and Agency Costs. A firm, whether public or private, is a legal entity defined by a set of contracts between resource owners who are cooperating within the framework of the firm. Those contracts specify, among other things, the rights and responsibilities of resource owners regarding such things as the division of labor, the sources of capital, and the ownership of residual earnings of the firm. The legal owners of the firm are typically those who have property rights in firm-specific physical assets.[4]

The term *property rights* refers not to a single right, but to a set or bundle of rights granted to firm owners. The specifics of the bundle of rights constituting ownership determine the nature of the institution. If, for example, property rights are restricted to one individual, then the firm is a sole proprietorship. If property rights are restricted to several people, the company is a partnership. If the property rights are freely transferable to anyone at low cost, the firm is an open corporation, or what we normally think of as the large, modern corporation. The bundle of rights defining the institution determines the mechanisms available to owners in controlling agency costs.[5]

Generally, ownership of any asset consists of three elements: (1) the right to use the asset, (2) the right to appropriate the returns on the asset, and (3) the right to change its form, substance, and location.[6] Within the context of a firm, the first element translates into an exclusive right, or exclusivity. The second translates into the right to the net cash flows of the firm, that is, the right to be a residual claimant. The third element implies that the owner has the right to transfer ownership of the share to another party, or transferability, as well as specific control rights over how the firm is run.

In contrast, ownership rights in a government-owned entity like the Postal Service are *public* property rights. Those rights are demonstrably different from private property rights when analyzed in the context of the three elements identified above. First, the public property right is not exclusive. There is common ownership based on citizenship. It is impossible to claim one's own portion of firm equity. Second, the firm's owners, citizen-taxpayers, are not given direct ownership rights to the net cash flows of the firm. They are not residual claimants, either de facto or de jure.[7] Third, the ownership right is not transferable: no market and thus no price exist for those rights. The latter fact causes particularly egregious problems in corporate governance.

The citizen-owners of a government firm thus have rights associated with ownership only in the weak sense that they can transfer them by changing citizenship, obtain residual cash flows through tax reductions or rebates (and bear residual losses through deficits or tax increases), and affect resource allocation decisions (for example, investment and financing) through an indirect voting-to-bureaucracy mechanism. Because fewer rights are associated with ownership in government corporations, ownership rights are severely attenuated relative to private ownership.

Due to the nature of the property rights held by owners of private firms, a wide variety of market-based mechanisms is available to private owners in monitoring managers. The mechanisms exist mainly because the transferable nature of private ownership shares (or residual claims) effectively lowers the cost of monitoring. They can usefully be grouped into those external versus those internal to the firm.

External Control Mechanisms. The transferability aspect of private ownership rights is critical for the creation of several important managerial control mechanisms in modern corporations. When combined with rights to residual cash flows, transferability provides not only the ability but also the incentive to control managers effectively. Transferability and residual claimancy form the basis for markets in ownership rights from which several control mechanisms stem, including stock prices, debt ratings, ownership concentration, and takeovers. All those mechanisms exist in private but not in government-owned corporations.

Stock prices derive directly from the transferable nature of private ownership shares because transferability allows a market, which continuously prices or values the right, to be established in those rights. Stock prices provide useful but inexpensive signals about the effectiveness of current management in maximizing owners' wealth. They quickly reflect the market's expectation regarding the effect of managerial decisions on current and future net cash flows. Owners do not need to be experts in analyzing the efficacy of managerial decisions to discern probable effects on future cash flows; they need only observe the firm's stock price. Large abnormal changes in share values lead to abnormal gains or losses for shareholders, who thus have an incentive to hold managers accountable for unusual returns. The stock price mechanism exerts considerable pressure, both externally and internally, on management to contain agency costs and operate the firm in the interest of owners. Numerous empirical studies support the proposition that stock markets help solve agency problems. Managerial removals are correlated with negative abnormal stock returns. Managerial pay packages are often structured so as to correlate managerial wealth with stockholder wealth, as reflected by stock returns.[8]

Most organizations that issue tradable stock also issue debt. Capital structures comprised of either all equity or all debt are rarely observed. Stated differently, the issuance of publicly held debt is often associated with transferable ownership shares. One reason is that the issuance of publicly traded debt helps to lower agency costs through the specialized evaluation of default risk.[9] That benefit will not accrue for firms receiving government-guaranteed debt.

Banks that issue credit to private companies specialize in the evaluation of default risk. The granting, denial, and interest rate given on a credit line provide information to owners about the risk of a firm's investment decisions. Banks frequently review the efficacy of their credit decisions and constantly update the information. Firms often pay for, and subsequently advertise, bank confirmation of a credit line that they do not use; their action suggests the market value of that information.[10]

Perhaps more important, large corporations often purchase ratings of publicly held debt from rating agencies (such as Moody's, Dunn & Bradstreet, and Standard & Poor's). Those agencies have a powerful incentive to maintain the integrity of their ratings. Bond ratings play a role similar to bank debt in the monitoring of investment risk and are readily available to both bond and stockholders. The specialized evaluation of default risk on debt lowers agency costs because owners can observe ratings on debt issues to infer the quality of managerial investment decisions, rather than engage in costly and specialized evaluation themselves.

Debt ratings by banks and others provide an important check on careless investment decisions by managers and thus constrain them to undertake only those projects within a risk category that owners find acceptable. Like the signaling value to owners of abnormal stock returns, abnormal variation in bond prices provides owners with market assessments of the risk of that firm's debt. Clearly that debt helps to lower the cost of managerial monitoring by owners.

Changes in the concentration of ownership in the modern corporation are also important for managerial monitoring. The benefits and costs of that concentration endogenously determine the concentration of ownership in a firm with tradable residual claims. If ownership shares are diffusely held, then no single owner has the incentive to monitor managers intensively. As ownership becomes more concentrated, however, single owners with increasing incentives to monitor managers carry the benefits and costs of monitoring.[11] The limiting case of total ownership concentration is sole proprietorship, in which monitoring costs are zero and the problem of agency costs is solved.[12]

Because ownership in private firms can become more concentrated as the benefits from concentration increase, we expect the intensity of managerial monitoring to increase as well. Concentration thus varies in ways that are consistent with the maximization of firm value. By allowing ownership concentration to increase with the benefits of more intensive monitoring, the transferability of ownership shares provides an additional monitoring device. If shareholders expect a wealth gain from greater monitoring, they can alter concentration accordingly. That action is not possible in government-owned firms because it is not possible to accumulate blocks of shares.

Takeovers are also a crucial mechanism for controlling agency costs. The transferability of ownership shares implies that management teams, using takeovers, can compete for control of firm assets through the purchase of stock. Competing management teams can circumvent entrenched boards and managers and gain control of a firm's decision process by purchasing the voting rights that attach to the firm's common stock. Control changes can occur through tender offers or proxy contests.

Takeovers are a costly but effective way of allowing competition among management teams for control of assets and thus ensuring that assets are employed in their highest valued use.[13] Such competition implies that management teams will be replaced when the cost of their inefficiency exceeds the transactions costs of a takeover. The market for corporate control disciplines managers to use the firm's assets effectively in the maximization of its value. Empirical evidence supports the hypothesis that takeovers operate to maximize shareholder wealth.[14] Because it is impossible to acquire their shares, takeovers of government-owned firms are not feasible.[15]

Internal Control Mechanisms. Internal mechanisms can also control agency costs. Their effectiveness also relates to the transferability of ownership shares. I briefly discuss two key internal control mechanisms: managerial pay packages and managerial turnover.

Corporate contractual arrangements allow the board of directors to determine the pay of a senior manager. Pay packages typically include salary, bonus, stock options, and restricted stock and are designed to align a senior manager's compensation with stockholders' wealth. Empirical evidence shows that managerial pay varies with returns to stock ownership.[16] If owners are dissatisfied with managerial performance, they can reduce managerial wealth directly by selling their shares; the sale will reduce the share price by imparting new information to the market. There is no need to go through an elected representative.

That control mechanism stems directly from the transferability of private ownership shares. As long as the firm has an effective incentive-pay package in place (which is a main function of the board), its owners need not rely solely on the board of directors to affect managerial wealth by directly adjusting executive compensation. Through stock, options, and restricted stock ownership, managerial pay is rapidly adjusted to performance at relatively low cost. Managerial pay tied to owner wealth is an important device for controlling agency costs.

The firing or retention of senior managers by the board depending on changes in stockholder wealth is another obvious way to reduce agency problems. The threat of firing during periods of poor firm performance encourages managers to act in the interests of owners. In private firms the board can use both accounting returns and stock returns as measures of owner wealth in its decision to retain or fire senior managers. Empirical evidence is consistent with the proposition that the CEO removals are correlated with owner wealth.[17]

Government Ownership and the Agency Problem. The bundle of rights associated with government ownership, that is, ownership by taxpayers of the assets of government firms, differs substantially from that of private ownership. That difference profoundly affects the mechanisms available to citizen-owners in controlling agency costs. The attenuation of rights inherent in public ownership causes a significant reduction in the availability of control mechanisms. Below I discuss how government ownership affects both internal and external managerial control mechanisms.

Because government-owned firms by definition do not have ownership shares that are tradable, the effectiveness of external control mechanisms is diminished. Nontransferability raises the cost of external control to prohibitively high levels. Ownership rights are not priced or valued on a market specializing in the trading of those rights. The cost of managerial monitoring is increased greatly because the effect of managerial decisions on future cash flows, and hence on firm value, cannot be discerned through stock prices. If a citizen-owner wishes to predict the effect of a manager's decision on firm value, he must invest time, effort, and knowledge in forming the forecast himself, rather than simply watching the reaction of the firm's stock price or bond rating to the decision. The fact that the owner's personal stake in the value of the government-owned firm is minuscule decreases the likelihood that such efforts will be undertaken.[18] The free-rider problem associated with the monitoring of managers by owners is greatly exacerbated by government ownership. Additionally, governmental, rather than managerial, actions that affect the firm are likely to increase monitoring costs. With high costs of monitoring and low benefits, managerial decisions are more likely to go unscrutinized.

The lack of pricing of property rights also implies that the benefits of monitoring to citizen-owners are reduced for another important reason: owners cannot directly capture the benefits from more effective monitoring through a higher share price. Capitalization of the future consequences of current monitoring through a higher current price of the right is impossible because the right is not traded and priced on a market. Owners have less incentive to monitor, and the equilibrium level of monitoring of public managers is relatively low.

Government-owned firms do not issue debt that is bonded by the firm's net cash inflows. Instead tax revenues of the relevant jurisdiction guarantee its debt. Therefore the capital market does not provide discipline through debt assessment for any financing activity conducted by government managers unless those decisions materially affect the ability of the jurisdiction to extract tax revenue. Ratings assigned to government-issued debt more likely reflect the willingness of the jurisdiction to tax citizens to repay bondholders than the prudence of managerial investment decisions per se. Relative to private firms, debt ratings of government firms provide poor information about the prudence of managerial decisions and thus raise the cost of managerial monitoring through that mechanism.

Hostile takeovers of government-owned firms are impossible because tradable residual claims do not exist. Owners are not able to buy shares on a market with the intention of replacing entrenched managers. The lack of transferability implies that it is more costly for competing management teams hoping to gain control of the decision process to do so: the disciplining effect on managers of tender offers, mergers, and proxy fights is nil.

Public ownership implies that control rights are retained through the vote, which allows public owners to affect agency costs only by means of their elected representatives. In a manner analogous to the election of boards of directors, owners can elect representatives who are committed to controlling agency costs in government firms. Those representatives can then pressure managers to operate the firm efficiently.

Such internal control mechanisms seem less effective in public firms for several reasons. First, by representation through elected representatives, two additional layers of agency are created: one between the voter and the representative and another between the representative and the board member. Second, representatives are elected to represent owners on a variety of issues, not just whom they appoint to the postal board of governors. Board members are less likely to represent accurately the intensity of owners' concerns about agency costs than the board member of a private firm, whose primary focus is overseeing the decision process of that firm. Third, members of the board of a private corporation are often experts in overseeing a firm's decision process and can be chosen for their specialized human capital. Because elected representatives are concerned with a variety of issues, they are less likely to have firm-specific information or to be experts in overseeing a firm's decisionmaking process than are elected members of the board of directors of a private firm. For those reasons boards of public firms are less effective in controlling agency costs than boards of private corporations.

Nothing in the public property structure of government enterprises prevents the internal control mechanisms of incentive pay or managerial turnover from operating per se.[19] Managerial wealth (and turnover) can be tied to accounting measures of owner wealth through incentive-pay packages.[20] Although accounting measures of profit may be poor measures of economic profit and hence owner wealth,[21] the public–property-rights structure of government enterprises makes other measures unavailable. It is not possible to tie incentive pay packages and managerial turnover to abnormal stock returns in a government firm because ownership shares do not trade. And because managerial incentive mechanisms cannot be linked to the price of tradable residual claims, no direct feedback mechanism, such as the stock price, exists by which owners express their preferences concerning governance of a firm. In government-owned enterprises dissatisfied owners cannot directly affect managerial wealth.

Relative to private firms, the citizen-owners of government enterprises have fewer mechanisms at their disposal to control agency costs. Citizens must rely on relatively ineffective internal control mechanisms to contain agency costs. Government-owned enterprises are consequently less effective institutions for monitoring managers than private firms. That trait manifests itself through managerial behavior that is not in the public interest. It may include excessive job perks, excessive job security, and accommodation of the interests of well-organized pressure groups that stand to expropriate the firm's residual. Because the creation of transferable ownership shares will likely improve the monitoring of postal management and reduce agency costs, it is in the public interest to create such tradable residual claims.

Another, often overlooked, reason exists to create transferable residual claims. The creation of such claims clearly defines who has a property right to the residual and thus clarifies the firm's objective: to maximize the value of that property right.[22] Scholars in law and economics have noted the importance of the shareholder wealth maximization criterion for corporate governance. For example, Jeffrey N. Gordon writes:

> The shareholder criterion is important not only because it gives guidance to managers about their role, but also because it implies a series of governance structures for the firm: for example, a board of directors selected exclusively by shareholder vote, and a set of fiduciary duties running from the board and the managers exclusively to the shareholders. Managers internalize the shareholder criterion as guiding and legitimating their actions (subject only to concerns about their own interests, the so-called "agency costs" problem). It tells them what to do in the event of a conflict between shareholder interests and those of other potential claimants on the firm, such as employees, suppliers, or communities. It also helps managers resolve conflicts among shareholders who may be differently situated in time preference or risk preference. Insofar as shares trade on well-developed markets, managers may observe the shareholder criterion simply by maximizing the stock price.[23]

The creation of a clear set of fiduciary duties is crucial for the Postal Service because one of its recurring problems has been vagueness about whom it is to serve, which results in various politically influential groups expropriating the residual. For example, John Tierney notes:

> Like most government agencies, the Postal Service has many constituencies it must satisfy—the general public, residents of rural areas, the organization's own large and politically powerful work force, and businesses that rely heavily on mail service in their operations (including magazine publishers, direct-mail advertisers, and mail-order companies).[24]

Those groups have been able to exploit the Postal Service's lack of focus and use its monopoly power and government ownership to their own advantage—and essentially have become the de facto residual claimants of the firm. It is unclear why serving those groups' particular

interest is in the broader public interest. The creation of tradable residual claims would effectively take such political concerns out of the Postal
Service and thus achieve another key goal of the 1970 act. In addition to
ameliorating the agency problem, the creation of tradable residual claims
immediately clarifies the firm's objectives.

Successful Deregulation of Network Industries
in the United States

A second reason to believe that postal reform is in the public interest
stems from the record of successful deregulation of a wide range of network industries in the United States, including trucking, railroads,
telecommunications, airlines, cable television, banking, and natural
gas.[25] Those industries share a common network structure with postal
services, as John Panzer states:

> Like telecommunications, electric power, and most transportation,
> postal service is a *network industry*. While postal service does not
> exhibit the *sunk costs* associated with those industries, its network
> structure has important implications for the analysis of efficient
> industry structure in the market for postal services.[26]

Network industries are usually distinguished by the fact that they
use distribution systems of lines, pipes, or routes requiring the use of
public rights of way, typically with strong physical linkages between
component parts. Many have substantial fixed costs and were once
widely considered to be natural monopolies requiring detailed regulation.

A wave of deregulation begun in the mid-1970s swept away some
of the most restrictive regulatory structures created in the United States
in the late nineteenth and early twentieth centuries. Much of that
deregulation was in network industries. Regulated industries produced
17 percent of U.S. GNP in 1977, but by 1988 the share had fallen to
6.6 percent.[27]

The Interstate Commerce Commission, for example, began to liber-
alize trucking rates in the late 1970s. Senator Edward Kennedy, consumer

advocate Ralph Nader, and many others realized that the deregulation of trucking was beneficial to consumers. A wide coalition supported the Motor Carrier Reform Act of 1980, which codified many of the ICC's actions and caused substantial deregulation of trucking.

In another example the Natural Gas Policy Act of 1978 began deregulation of the natural gas industry. The act created a timetable for deregulating the wellhead price of most natural gas.[28] The wellhead price of all natural gas discovered after 1976 was deregulated in 1985. Starting in 1985, the Federal Energy Regulatory Commission allowed open access in natural gas, which created competitive gas markets in which customers could deal directly with gas suppliers. Pipelines were converted into transporters of natural gas. Interstate pipelines have remained regulated according to traditional rate-of-return principles, but all other sectors of the industry have been effectively deregulated. Similar regulatory reforms occurred in a wide variety of other industries.

Evidence on the effects of deregulation of network industries in the United States is favorable and suggests that postal reform is likely to yield substantial net social benefits. I review deregulation's effects in six industries that most reflect the Postal Service's network structure, including natural gas, airlines, trucking, telecommunications, cable television, and railroads.[29]

In 1993 Clifford Winston of the Brookings Institution conducted a survey of studies of the predicted and actual effects of regulatory reform in nine industries.[30] He compiled estimates of deregulation's effects across a vast literature and presented the range of estimates in the form of billions of annual 1990 U.S. dollars. Here I convert Winston's estimates into 1999 dollars and report them for industries selected for their similarity to postal services.

Robert Crandall and Jerry Ellig recently summarized a large body of evidence on five industries (natural gas, telecommunications, airlines, railroads, and trucking) and examined evidence on price, quantity, and quality.[31] Those estimates are also relevant for postal services. The experience with U.S. deregulation suggests that substantial inefficiencies were created under regulation for a variety of reasons and that the introduction of competition eliminated those inefficiencies.

Effects of Regulatory Reform on Prices and Service. Crandall and Ellig conducted a thorough review of the effects of deregulation on several network industries. They found that real prices broadly declined after reform. In terms of percentage declines in airline fares, they noted that yields (the average amount of revenue received per passenger mile), which analysts commonly use by to measure fare trends, declined:

> The average yield fell from 21.65 cents in 1977 to 13.76 cents in 1995, a 37-percent reduction. Much of this decline occurred during the first 10 years of deregulation, when the yield fell by 29 percent, from $21.65 to $15.32. Interestingly, yields fell almost immediately in response to deregulation.[32]

They also documented the fall in natural gas prices after deregulation. Adjusting for inflation, they found that wellhead prices fell by 60 percent between 1984 and 1995. They discovered that the prices paid by various classes of consumers (for example, residential, commercial, electric utility) also decreased significantly.[33] Regarding interstate telecommunications rates, they found that after the AT&T divestiture in 1984, the consumer price index for interstate long-distance rates decreased from approximately 60 in 1984 to about 30 today.[34] The intrastate rates have also fallen, but somewhat less rapidly.

Table 5-1 summarizes Crandall and Ellig's findings on price change in five network industries two, five, and ten years after deregulation. Changes in first-class and total real mail rates for similar periods are displayed for comparison. Over a five-year period, prices in deregulated industries decreased, from 3 percent (for trucking) to 45 percent (for natural gas). For postal services, in contrast, real prices *increased* 2.07 percent for first-class and 2.40 percent for total mail prices for a similar five-year period. For the ten-year period, prices in deregulated industries declined more uniformly, from 27 to 57 percent (both for natural gas). Postal rates increased 0.007 percent for first-class and 4.12 percent for total mail prices for a similar period.[35] The data suggest that regulatory reform provided substantial benefits to consumers in deregulated industries but that postal customers did not enjoy similar benefits over the period.

Table 5-1 Summary of Price Changes from Regulatory Reform in the United States

Industry	Real Price Change		
	After 2 years	After 5 years	After 10 years
Natural gas	decline of 10–38% (1984–1986)	decline of 23–45% (1984–1989)	decline of 27–57% (1984–1994)
Long-distance telecommunications	decline of 5–16% (1984–1986)	decline of 23–41% (1984–1989)	decline of 40–47% (1984–1994)
Airlines	decline of 13% (1977–1979)	decline of 12% (1977–1982)	decline of 29% (1977–1997)
Trucking	NA	decline of 3–17% (1980–1985)	decline of 28–56% (1977–1987)
Railroads	decline of 4% (1980–1982)	decline of 20% (1980–1984)	decline of 44% (1980–1990)
Mail prices, selected years			
real first-class mail prices	decline of 0.025% (1984–1986)	increase of 2.07% (1984–1989)	increase of 0.007% (1984–1994)
real overall mail prices	decline of 0.14% (1984–1986)	increase of 2.40% (1984–1989)	increase of 4.12% (1984–1994)

SOURCE: Robert W. Crandall and Jerry Ellig, *Economic Deregulation and Customer Choice: Lessons for the Electric Utility Industry* (Center for Market Processes 1997), p. 2; *Annual Report of the Postmaster General*, various years.

Rather than reporting price changes in terms of percentages, Winston normalized the savings to consumers into billions of 1990 dollars per year. Adjusting with the consumer price index, table 5-2 reports those values in 1999 dollars. I summarize Winston's estimates of the effect of the wave of regulatory reform in the 1970s on prices and, in some cases, service levels in five industries. A positive number in column 3 indicates a gain for consumers due to lower prices or improved service. With the exception of the lowest estimates for railroads, U.S. consumers uniformly benefited from deregulation. Airline customers gained $5.5–8.3 billion per year through lower fares from deregulation of airlines. They gained approximately $10.8 billion from greater frequency of service but lost almost $4 billion from increased travel restrictions. Significant gains for trucking customers were also recorded. Natural gas was also assessed, but results were reported simply as "substantial gains to consumers." The findings suggest that postal customers would likely gain billions of dollars per year through the increased competition brought about by postal reform.

Effects of Regulatory Reform on Profits. Examining groups other than consumers is important. Economic theory yields conflicting predictions about how deregulation is likely to affect profits. Deregulation may reduce profits because prices were set above marginal cost in most industries so that competition would reduce revenues and thus profits.[36] Alternatively insulation from competition is likely to raise costs due to inefficient operation so that the introduction of competition would lower costs and thus increase profits. Clifford Winston summarizes this second view, which seems particularly relevant for postal services:

> First, an old-fashioned view is that regulation improves welfare because it helps control monopoly. This view has been discredited because it is clear that regulation primarily limits competition among firms, and this lack of competition causes an industry to accumulate substantial managerial slack or "X-inefficiency"; that is, firms do not minimize the cost of producing a given level of output. When an industry is deregulated, unrestricted competition among incumbent firms and from new entrants forces the industry to shed such inefficiencies and to seek out innovations in marketing, operations, and technology.[37]

Winston reported the effects of regulatory reform on profits, summarized in table 5-3 in billions of 1999 dollars annually. Positive numbers represent profit gains.

Table 5-3 indicates that most industries experienced a profit gain, or at least no large losses, from deregulation, with airlines enjoying the largest gain of $6.25 billion annually. The trucking industry is

Table 5-2 Summary of the Assessed Effects of Regulatory Reform on Prices and Service

Industry	Affected Areas	Outcome ($ billions)
Airlines	fares	(5.48, 8.29)
	service frequency	10.84
	travel restrictions	-3.82
Trucking	common carrier rates	9.94
	private carrier rates	7.65
Long-distance telecommunications	rates	(0.93, 2.04)
Cable TV	price and service	(0.47, 1.66)
Railroads	rates	(-2.68, 0.55)

SOURCE: Clifford Winston, "Economic Deregulation: Days of Reckoning for Microeconomists," *Journal of Economic Literature* 31 (1993): 1274–75. Positive values indicate consumer gains. Values are in billions of 1999 dollars.

Table 5-3 Summary of the Assessed Effects of Regulatory Reform on Profits

Industry	Outcome (in billions of dollars)
Airlines	6.25
Trucking	-6.12
Long-distance telecommunications	small change
Cable TV	increase
Railroads	4.08

Source: Clifford Winston, "Economic Deregulation: Days of Reckoning for Microeconomists," *Journal of Economic Literature* 31 (1993): 1278–79. Positive values indicate a profit gain. Values are in billions of 1999 dollars.

anomalous: it lost $6.12 billion in profits annually from deregulation. In general the cost-reducing effect of competition appears to dominate the revenue-reducing effect, and consumer gains come not from reductions in owners' wealth, but rather from net efficiency improvements.

The effect of de-monopolization on profits in postal services would likely be more profound for at least two reasons. First, no residual claimants have ever existed for postal services de jure; incentives for profit maximization have never existed. Second, postal services have been a government-owned monopoly for a much longer time than any of the other industries; inefficiencies are likely to be more imbedded in its institutional structure.

Effects of Regulatory Reform on Wages and Employment. A possible rejoinder is that consumers and stockholders benefited from deregulation at the expense of workers. Massive cuts in wages and employment could result in reduced prices and increased profits—and a general welfare loss. Table 5-4 presents Winston's summary of the estimates of deregulation's effect on wages and employment.

Although airlines experienced a small decline in wages, deregulation in that sector led to an increase in employment, probably because of increased frequency of flights. Trucking experienced a decline in both wages and employment, which, together with the profit decline, suggests that firms and workers shared lost monopoly rents.[38] Railroad workers also suffered a substantial decline in wages, although employment was not affected. Cable television, like the airlines, actually experienced an increase in employment.

One interpretation of those data is that deregulation of postal services will result in a slight reduction in wages but an actual increase in industry employment. A decline in postal wages under regulatory reform would be consistent with the evidence on a positive postal wage premium. Expanding private express services, however, may rapidly hire postal workers because of their specialized knowledge of routes, address locations, methods of sorting, and other delivery technologies.[39] Moreover, if prices fall under postal reform as seems likely due to substantial efficiency improvements, then the entire postal sector will

Table 5-4 Summary of the Assessed Effects of Regulatory Reform on Wages and Employment

Industry	Affected Areas	Outcome ($ billions)
Airlines	wages employment	small decline increase of 6%
Trucking	wages employment	(-1.4, -2.42) decline
Long-distance telecommunications	wages (communicaton) wages (equipment)	no change decline
Cable TV	wages employment	no assessment increase
Railroads	wages employment	decline of 20% no effect

SOURCE: Clifford Winston, "Economic Deregulation: Days of Reckoning for Microeconomists," *Journal of Economic Literature* 31 (1993): 1282. Positive values indicate a gain to labor. Values are in billions of 1990 dollars.

expand, with increasing employment as a result. That outcome is consistent with the experience in other similar industries.

Given that some groups may benefit while others lose, it is important to consider the net effects of deregulation. Table 5-5 reports the findings on the general effects of regulatory reform in the United States. The table sums the effects on both consumers and producers to obtain the net effect of deregulation in that industry. Positive numbers in the total column indicate that deregulation in general produced a welfare gain. For all industries examined, the net effect was clearly positive and indicates that consumer gains outweighed any welfare losses suffered by producers or employees (for example, trucking companies). Net gains imply improvements in economic efficiency, most captured by consumers. Winston noted that when total gains are summed across industries, social welfare improved by at least $46–59 billion annually from deregulation.[40] Benefits from reform of the massive postal industry are likely to be substantial as well.

Table 5-5 Summary of the Assessed Effects of Regulatory Reform

Industry	Consumers	Producers	Total
Airlines	(11.22, 18.87)	6.25	(17.72, 25.11)
Trucking	19.63	-6.12	13.51
Long-distance telecommunications	(0.93, 2.04)	—	(0.93, 2.04)
Cable TV	(0.47, 1.66)	—	(0.47, 1.66)
Railroads	(9.18, 12.37)	4.08	(13.26, 16.44)

SOURCE: Clifford Winston, "Economic Deregulation: Days of Reckoning for Microeconomists," *Journal of Economic Literature* 31 (1993): 1284. Positive values indicate a gain. Values are in billions of 1999 dollars per year.

Additional Margins of Adjustment

The above estimates indicate that substantial net social gains were realized from reform of network industries in the United States. Deregulated industries, however, have continued to adjust to competition over time (and are in all likelihood still adjusting) in a variety of unanticipated ways, many difficult to measure precisely. Adjustments include improved marketing techniques, adoption of more efficient technologies, improved operations, more effective corporate governance, more flexibility in responding to external shocks, heightened service quality, the introduction of more new products, and increased responsiveness to customer's needs.[41] The evidence indicates that managers are younger, better educated, and more entrepreneurial in a deregulated environment.[42]

The above estimates thus likely understate the true magnitude of the long-term net social gains from regulatory reform. As Clifford Winston suggests, such additional adjustment was, on reflection, predictable:

> It is not surprising that deregulated (or partially deregulated) industries are slow to achieve maximum efficiency. When regulatory restrictions on pricing, operations, and entry (especially from new

firms), have been enforced for decades, managers and employees of regulated firms settle into patterns of inefficient production and missed opportunities for technological advance and entry into new markets.[43]

Such an underestimate is particularly pertinent for U.S. postal services, where entry has been prohibited not for decades, but for centuries. Inefficient patterns of production are surely more deeply ingrained. That factor suggests that the benefits of reform are likely to grow over a period of decades. Those long-term benefits should be factored into postal policy decisions.

Some commentators may be reluctant to draw inferences about the likely effect of postal reform from deregulation in other industries. Winston, however, suggested that the experience across industries has been remarkably similar: "Industries are likely to behave quite similarly when it comes to adjusting to deregulation, and that their adjustment, while time-consuming, will raise consumer welfare—significantly even at first, and increasingly over time."[44]

Regulatory reform of network industries in the United States appears to have created substantial benefits for consumers as well as other groups. The social cost of rate and entry regulation, relative to competitive markets, seems substantially higher than previously thought. The long-term social benefits of regulatory reform of U.S. postal services may produce even greater gains because it is likely to be a highly competitive industry, has low fixed costs, is government-owned, and has been protected from competition for centuries.

Technological Change and the Case for Reform

Chapter 3 noted that the two main explanations for government intervention in postal services are universal service, meaning subsidized delivery to rural areas, and natural monopoly. I provided several reasons to question those justifications. In this section I discuss how technological change is further weakening those rationales for government intervention and making postal reform even more imperative.

Although I discuss relatively recent technological developments, technological change eliminated the need for a government-provided post more than 100 years ago. The term *postal service* originally referred to transportation using a series of posts, or relay stations, that typically housed men and horses: "Letters were conveyed either by 'through post,' that is, by means of a single rider who obtained fresh horses at each station, or by 'standing post,' that is, by a series of riders, each of whom handed the mail to a subsequent rider at the next station. A *foot post* was similar in concept but relied on walking messengers."[45] That process was considered a rapid form of transport in early America.

Significant advances in transportation, including the railroad and the steamboat, came about with the Industrial Revolution. Those technologies could transport large quantities of mail more rapidly than traditional posts, and entrepreneurs actively used them to carry mail. To confront that technological threat, the Post Office requested that Congress extend its monopoly to include postal control of railroad schedules. Congress responded by extending the postal monopoly to include intercity transport by private expresses through the Postal Act of 1845.[46] Technological threats to postal services are not new.

Technological Change in the Delivery of Printed Matter. Technological change has dramatically reduced the social benefits of a universal service network of physical mail delivery for at least two reasons. First, technological change has led to an important change in the composition of the mail toward bulk-mail advertising matter and away from personal messages. Second, technological change has increased the availability of, and drastically reduced the cost of, substitutes for letter communications and has thus virtually eliminated the possibility of rural customer isolation absent government-owned and monopolized mail.

Recent technological change in the process of handling printed matter has been dramatic. Optical character recognition has been central to the process. That technology, along with increased use of computerized barcoding of mail, has led to a highly automated process under which the USPS can process mail almost without human involvement.

Indeed some mail sorting centers are known as lights-out facilities because no human need attend to them.

Many pieces of commercial mail are now pre-barcoded by the sender. That process assists in mail sorting and delivery. For pieces without a barcode, the USPS maintains a remote barcoding system that is specifically designed, with the help of optical character readers, to barcode mail correctly. "Multiline optical character readers and facer cancelers" create a video image of the address, which is then processed by a "remote computer reader." A computer attempts to interpret the image electronically to affix the proper barcode. If it cannot, it automatically transmits the image to a "remote encoding center," where a human enters the address by hand.[47]

The technology has been successful in recognizing printed addresses but due to wide divergence in writing styles, less so in recognizing handwritten addresses. In 2000 the remote computer reader could correctly assess only about 2 percent of handwritten mail. Today it can recognize 25 percent. The USPS has contracted for software development that will soon result in a 50 percent recognition rate, which attests to the rapid pace of technological change.[48]

Additional technologies include robots on pedestals that assist with the loading and sorting of mail trays. The computerized mail-processing system allows the USPS to manage address changes more easily and supports upgrades in its mail-tracking capability. Moreover, the USPS authorized two private firms, e-Stamp Corporation and Stamps.com Inc., to sell digital postage online. Any computer user can print out an encrypted stamp image if he has established an online account with a postage vendor.[49]

Such developments promise to conserve relatively expensive postal labor costs. But the USPS readily admits that although those technological developments are likely to reduce the cost of mailing personal letters, they particularly favor the use of the mails for commercial purposes, that is, for mass mailings.[50] They facilitate the targeting of mail by zip code and other characteristics.

Evidence supports the view that USPS operations are becoming more commercially oriented. The USPS provides substantial discounts—

called work-sharing discounts—to large mailers that barcode and presort their material beforehand.[51] Large-scale mailers can more easily barcode and presort than individuals sending personal letters. Such discounts encourage the use of the mails by businesses, which frequently issue mass mailings for advertising purposes.

The changing composition of first-class mail provides additional evidence that the mail is increasingly commercial. In 1977, household-to-other-household mail was 12 percent of total first-class mail volume while non–household-to-household mail was 39 percent. By 1991 household-to-household decreased to 8.4 percent, while non–household-to-household increased to 44.3 percent.[52] Personal letters between citizens are a relatively small and decreasing component of monopolized first-class mail, while commercial mail is growing. The trend is consistent with technological change lowering the cost of commercial mailing.

Observing the ratio of first-class to third-class revenues can give a rough measure of the effect. First-class mail includes personal correspondence and postcards (and also a significant amount of commercial mail). Standard mail A (formerly third-class mail) is primarily business mail. The Postal Service defines that category as "formerly called third-class mail, Standard Mail (A) generally includes letters, flats and parcels that do not require the security of First-Class Mail nor the speed of Priority Mail. Advertisers or others generally mailing identical pieces of mail in bulk use this class of mail which makes up almost 22 percent of our revenue."[53] Figure 5-1 shows the change in the ratio from 1971 to the present. The ratio generally remained above 4 until 1983. In recent years it hit a low of 2.6. The shift suggests that the across-class (as well as the within-class) composition of the Postal Service's revenue stream has also moved away from personal letters and cards and toward more commercial mail.

The monopoly is defended as a way of protecting delivery of printed matter to rural customers. But is the intention to ensure that rural customers are guaranteed delivery of mass-produced advertising matter? The evidence indicates that technology is increasingly moving the composition of mail flows in that direction. Defenders of the postal monopoly must now argue that without the cross-subsidy, rural citizens would somehow

Figure 5-1 Ratio of First-Class to Third-Class Mail Revenues, 1971–1997

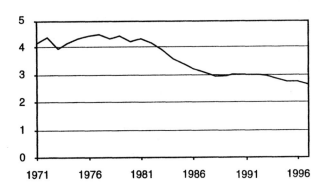

become isolated from the larger society if they did not receive (or received at higher cost to the mailer) mass-produced advertising matter.

Technological developments are moving the Postal Service further from the core activity on which the traditional case for government monopoly is based: delivery of personal letters to rural areas. To the extent that is true, the case for a legally enforced monopoly is weakened. Technological progress in substitutes for letter communications, which also reduces the likelihood that rural residents will become isolated, has been even more profound.

Technological Change in Substitutes for Letter Communications. Unlike colonial times, today letters are only one communication method among many. The alternatives in communication have burgeoned, while the costs have declined. One obvious alternative is the telephone. Many country dwellers may find a phone call more effective in preventing isolation than a letter because a call allows direct interaction. Cellular phones are much more widely available. Crandall and Ellig have shown that real long-distance telephone rates fell anywhere from 40 to 47 percent between 1984 and 1994. As technological advance-ment continues to reduce the price of phone calls, rural citizens will find the phone an increasingly viable alternative to communication by letter.

Another alternative is the facsimile, a close substitute for letters in that a written message can be transmitted instantaneously at low cost. Transmission costs have been falling with telephone rates. Although both sender and receiver must have access to a fax machine to complete the communication, numerous businesses are willing to provide those services, and inexpensive fax machines are widely available. For time-sensitive communications in which a hard copy is preferable, the speed of that form surpasses traditional letter mail.

The most formidable technological substitute for letter delivery is electronic mail. That form of communication allows written messages to be transmitted instantaneously, but at much lower cost than letters. Once both sender and receiver have access to a computer, the marginal cost to them of sending and receiving a message is close to zero. The advent of computers designed strictly for Internet access has lowered the cost of using that medium. Given the rapid rate of technological change in the computer industry, the costs of accessing a computer and of sending electronic mail messages will fall still further. Rural residents have an added incentive to substitute into electronic mail, since it provides a fast and convenient method of interacting where cost is unrelated to distance. Frank A. Wolak, an economist at Stanford University, estimated that annual increases in the use of household personal computers at historical rates would result in reductions in spending by households on postal services at least as large as those resulting from a 10 percent increase in postal rates.[54]

Moreover, the delivery of electronic mail is to a logical address, which allows the mail to be retrieved wherever there is an Internet connection, rather than a physical address: electronic mail is more accessible. The advent of direct broadcast satellite (DBS) technology, which provides wireless access to the Internet, makes electronic mail still more accessible. At least 1 million customers get high-speed Internet connections in this manner.[55] Because a satellite's beam is ubiquitous, DBS technology allows universal communications and represents a clear improvement over rural delivery of physical mail.

The Postal Service has recognized that alternative technologies represent substantial competition in its two major classes of mail. In discussing first-class mail the USPS states, "This class of mail faces competition from electronic mail, facsimiles and automatic bill payment systems."[56] And for standard mail A: "This product faces competition from newspapers, television and mass faxing. The Internet has also emerged as a potentially strong competitor for the revenue generated by Standard Mail (A). The efficiencies of Internet advertising, especially the ability to reach specific groups, will have a significant impact in coming years."[57] Postmaster General Henderson stated:

> In theory, we should be on top of the world. In reality, we are facing a world of competition. This includes new inroads from traditional competitors, a slew of start-up delivery firms associated with the Internet, liberalized foreign posts that have opened offices in the United States and purchased American subsidiaries, and the accelerating growth of electronic alternatives to the mail.[58]

Given the wide variety of highly competitive substitutes, one wonders why it is necessary to retain a government monopoly to guarantee service to rural communities. The available substitute technologies have multiplied significantly since the eighteenth century. Postal services are a different good from electricity, for example, in which few adequate substitutes exist. The number and declining price of the options rural customers now have for keeping in touch suggest that it is unwarranted to claim that, if the cross-subsidy were eliminated and rural customers had to pay the full cost of deliveries to them, they would become isolated or otherwise significantly inconvenienced.

Technological Advancement and the Natural Monopoly Rationale. Several developments suggest that technology is weakening any natural monopoly aspect of postal services. First, to the extent that technological change is lowering the cost of providing delivery services through the increased efficiency of trucks and enhanced management of them through computerization, more competitors will enter the industry and compete for local delivery. The change will make the delivery market more contestable. That is, more firms and technologies are now available to threaten entry if prices exceed costs. That potential reduces concerns about natural monopoly.

Second, demand conditions will likely change with technology so that natural monopoly is no longer a concern. Average costs are unlikely to fall for all ranges of output in most industries. At some sufficiently high level of output, they rise or become constant as output increases. That trend is particularly true of postal services because fixed costs are relatively low compared with many other network industries. For any industry, as technology develops, the demand curve will more likely intersect the long-run average cost curve in its constant returns-to-scale portion.[59] That change occurs for three reasons. First, technological developments spur economic growth, which increases the demand for most goods, including postal services. Second, technology increases the number of available substitutes and makes the demand curve for postal services flatter, or more price-sensitive (that is, more elastic). That change also raises the likelihood that the constant-returns portion of the cost curve is the relevant portion. Third, technological change affects the cost curve itself and likely shifts it down. All those effects imply that a natural monopoly in postal services, if it ever existed, is merely a temporary phenomenon. As Viscusin, Vernon, and Harrington suggest, the railroad industry provides an example:

> This phenomenon is not rare. Railroads possessed significant cost advantages in the late 1800s, and these advantages were eroded considerably with the introduction of trucking in the 1920s. This example introduces a new element, namely, technological change. That is, over long periods of time it is likely that the cost function will shift as new knowledge is incorporated into the production process. Hence, permanent natural monopoly is probably a rare category. Technical change can shift cost functions so as to render competition workable.[60]

Just as trucking reduced the natural monopoly aspects of railroads, the increasing availability of substitutes for letter delivery, such as phone, facsimile machines, and electronic mail, are eliminating any natural monopoly in postal delivery that may now exist.

Summary

In this chapter I have reviewed three arguments for postal reform that are relatively underappreciated. First, postal reform that established transferable residual claims, as the Kappel commission envisioned, would result in the creation of numerous managerial control mechanisms that are now absent. Those include external mechanisms such as the use of stock prices to signal managerial performance, meaningful debt ratings, takeovers, and changes in ownership concentration, as well as internal mechanisms, including managerial pay related to firm performance and managerial turnover related to firm performance. The availability of those mechanisms would greatly reduce the agency costs of postal organization.

Second, the experience with deregulation of other industries similar in structure to postal services suggests that postal reform would create substantial net gains. The effects of deregulation of trucking, airlines, railroads, long-distance telecommunications, and cable television, among others, indicate that deregulation created billions of dollars of annual net value. Most of those gains were obtained through the introduction of competition, and increasing gains were realized over the long-term as industries continued to adjust to market forces. Gains are likely to be even greater for postal services because they are government-owned and have been monopolized for centuries.

Third, recent technological changes are weakening the case for government intervention in postal services. Technology is moving the composition of the mail stream away from personal letters toward more business advertising matter. Numerous substitutes—including telephones, cellular phones, facsimile machines, and electronic mail—are available to rural citizens for staying connected to the wider community. None of those alternatives were available when the Post Office was founded in the eighteenth century, and their cost is falling rapidly. The argument that rural citizens will be isolated without government-provided monopoly mail today rings hollow.

Additionally, technological change is weakening the natural monopoly argument for government intervention in postal services. Numerous competitors are prepared to enter various markets and make postal services highly contestable.

6

Global Postal Reform

The traditional organizational structure for postal services internationally has been a fully vertically integrated government-owned firm with a legally enforced monopoly over letter delivery. It has become increasingly clear that such an organizational structure is ill adapted to an environment of rapid technological change in communication services. For the wide variety of reasons discussed above, I conclude that the most appropriate institutional structure for postal services in the United States is a competitive industry offering tradable residual claims, or transferable property rights to the net cash flows from postal operations. Such a structure is in the public interest, and will better achieve the goals of the 1970 act.

Competition and transferable residual claims will give the Postal Service the incentive to maximize profits, which will lead the Postal Service to utilize the latest business methods, marketing techniques, most efficient delivery technologies, most effective corporate governance, highest service quality, and the newest products. Postal productivity will be enhanced. Because the Postal Service will face competition, it will have the incentive to pass cost savings along to consumers through lower prices. The drain on the Treasury through implicit and explicit postal subsidies will be eliminated. Postal delivery will instead contribute to the Treasury through increased tax revenue.

Governments around the world have reacted to technological change in communications services by modernizing their postal sectors. Postal reform is a truly global movement, and countries have taken a variety of approaches to restructuring. Reform has progressed more rapidly in some countries than in others. I here provide an overview of reform movements in ten countries. This section is intended not to provide an exhaustive discussion of the nuances of postal reform in every country,[1] but instead to provide a sense of how different countries have approached postal reform. The review also suggests that meaningful reform includes changes in ownership form and limitations on the postal monopoly.

New Zealand

New Zealand was the first country to begin significant postal reform—and it completely abolished its postal monopoly. In 1986 the New Zealand government transformed the New Zealand Post Office into New Zealand Post, a government-owned corporation. That reform was somewhat similar to the creation of the U.S. Postal Service in 1970, with the new entity government-owned and headed by a board of directors.

Unlike the 1970 reform, however, New Zealand undertook a meaningful evaluation of its monopoly statutes and subsequently introduced competition. Pending additional study, New Zealand initially limited its postal monopoly to NZ$1.75 with a weight limit of 500 grams (1.1 pounds) in 1987.[2] At the time NZ$1.75 was about 4.5 times the stamp price. A private competitor could carry a letter only if it charged more than NZ$1.75 or if the item weighed more than 500 grams. The reform created a clearly defined "reserved" or "protected" service for the government's postal monopoly. Numerous other countries have used that type of limitation on the postal monopoly. In 1988 the New Zealand government's review resulted in a recommendation to repeal the postal monopoly completely by gradually reducing the reserved area of service. That is, the monopoly's price limit was reduced in stages over several years.[3]

New Zealand Post opposed the elimination of its monopoly. It marshaled three arguments that have been used frequently against competition. First, private competitors might enter only highly profitable rural routes and leave unprofitable routes for New Zealand Post. That action would threaten uniform rates and might result in closing rural post offices. Second, New Zealand Post suggested that recent service improvements and its relatively low postage rates meant that reform was unnecessary. Third, it noted that because postal services already faced competition from many substitutes, including electronic mail, telephones, and facsimiles, deregulation was pointless.

The New Zealand government did not accept those arguments. In 1990 the government changed the postal law so that over a two-year period the price limit would be reduced further to NZ$0.80 and the weight limit to 200 grams. It also allowed New Zealand Post to close one-third of its post offices and to contract with local stores to provide counter operations. New Zealand Post increased its charge for home delivery to rural areas.

Due to a change in government and public complaint about changes in rural service, full deregulation did not come until 1998. The Postal Services Act of 1998 removed New Zealand Post's letter monopoly and permitted full competition.[4] In a "deed of understanding" between the government and New Zealand Post, the price of a standard letter was capped at NZ$0.45 for three years. There is an agreed frequency of deliveries to a specified number of points with no rural delivery fee.[5] The government requires that New Zealand Post continue to provide universal service, but it is not required to charge uniform rates. New Zealand Post also has some flexibility in service requirements. It must provide 95 percent of households with letter delivery service six days per week, 99.88 percent of households with service five or six days per week, and the rest at least one to four days per week.[6] The act also imposed certain service obligations on private operators.

As a result of reform, New Zealand Post has introduced services and has improved its efficiency without government support. "Since corporatization, NZP has modernized its technology, transportation network, and retail facilities and invested in subsidiary businesses, all funded by retained earning and the sale of surplus assets. By 1995, with 30 percent more mail to deliver, costs had been reduced by 30 percent, and labor productivity had doubled."[7] It reduced postage rates in 1995 from NZ$0.45 to NZ$.040, and the real price of a letter fell by almost 30 percent between 1987 and 1995. New Zealand Post has earned a profit every year since 1986 and earned NZ$21 million in 2000–2001.

Although New Zealand Post remains a government-owned firm, the effects of introducing competition have been positive. New Zealand Post has reduced its work force by 40 percent. It did so without major labor strife, primarily through the use of early retirement and other incentive packages.[8]

Australia

Through the Australian Postal Corporation Act of 1989, the Australian government converted its post office into a government-owned enterprise called Australia Post. Australia Post is required to operate commercially and to provide universal service at a uniform rate throughout Australia. A cross-subsidy explicitly funds the provision of universal service at an estimated cost of A$79 million in 1999.[9] Australia Post is subject to taxes and customs duties. The price limit on the postal monopoly was reduced from ten to four times the stamp price, with the weight limit reduced from 500 to 250 grams.

In July 1998 the government announced support for legislation that would further reduce the price limit on the postal monopoly to A$0.45, the same as the current stamp price. Private competitors could thus compete with Australia Post as long as they did not charge less than the stamp price itself. Those proposals for further deregulation of the letter market remain before the Australian Parliament.

As in New Zealand, the effects of reform have generally been positive. The basic postage rate has remained stable at A$0.45 for eight years, and Australia Post has earned profits in every year since 1987. On-time delivery has increased, and Australia Post has diversified into other businesses.

Finland

Finland was the first European country to abolish its postal monopoly. Finland Post, established in 1638, was part of PT Finland Group, comprised of both postal and telecommunications services. It has not held an exclusive right to convey personal messages since 1991. The Postal

Services Act of 1994 mandated that Finland Post become a limited liability company and that it provide nationwide delivery of mail, defined as an addressed item with a maximum weight of 2 kilograms.[10] Finland Post continued to operate as a government-owned enterprise.[11]

Finland Post supported reform because it viewed competition from new technologies as a greater threat than from liberalization. Its rates for competitive services (such as parcels and newspapers) are closely regulated.[12]

Sweden

Events in Sweden rapidly overshadowed the Finnish reforms. Sweden repealed its postal monopoly in 1992 rather than suppress CityMail, a new entrant in Stockholm. CityMail provided twice-weekly delivery of computer-generated mail in Stockholm. Sweden Post supported the elimination of its monopoly because it realized that without demonopolization it could not obtain the commercial flexibility needed to compete effectively.

Through the 1993 Postal Services Act, Sweden Post was converted into a government-owned stock company, which pays a value-added tax. The National Postal and Telecom Agency, a new regulator, was also established by the act. The 1993 act removed Sweden Post's mail monopoly. The postal monopoly was repealed as of January 1, 1993. Competitors can enter the delivery market but must be licensed. The responsibility for providing universal mail service rests not with Sweden Post, but with the Swedish government. Although the government has contracted with Sweden Post to provide universal mail service, it presumably could contract with others.

Norway

The Norwegian Post and Telecommunications Authority (PT) has the responsibility for regulating the country's postal market. The Postal Services Act of 1996, as amended in 1997 and 1999, limited the postal monopoly to the dispatch of addressed letters weighing less than 350 grams, with a maximum postage of five times the standard first-class letter postage as long as those letters do not contain books, magazines, catalogues, or newspapers.[13] Many distribution services, messenger, and transport companies offer competing services in the nonreserved area. Norway Post is subject to a licensing system administered by PT. Norway Post's license ensures that it provides universal service, that it complies with the provisions of the EU's postal directive, and that it provides equitable and nondiscriminatory access to its postal network.

Germany

Germany has undertaken postal reform through a sophisticated three-step plan. Postreform I, in 1989, resulted in the reorganization of the Ministry for Posts and Telecommunications. It separated postal services, postal banking, and telecommunications and created different departments for each. The department for postal services was named Deutsche Bundespost Postdienst. Management of Postdienst came from the department for postal services. A new board, with members from the private sector, was created to oversee the postal services department.

Postreform II, implemented in 1994, converted Postdienst into Deutsche Post A.G., a corporation with all shares owned by the government. It also amended the German constitution to guarantee "appropriate and adequate" universal postal services.

The German Parliament agreed to Postreform III in 1997. Through Postreform III, universal service is considered a responsibility of the German government, not an obligation of Deutsche Post. That distinction is critical because funds to provide for universal service need not come from markups on urban delivery, implicit tax subsidies, credit guarantees, or other sources. Instead those funds are obtained through revenues from licenses. All delivery services carrying addressed mail weighing less than 1,000 grams (2.2 pounds) must obtain a license. If the market does not provide universal service within the licensed area, then licensees may be required to provide basic postal service and are entitled to compensation for losses incurred. Compensation is to be paid from a fund composed of all licensees earning more than 1 million deutsche marks annually.

Postreform III also abolished the Ministry for Posts and Telecommunications and repealed the postal monopoly as of the end of 2002. That is, Postreform III granted Deutsche Post a monopoly on the carriage of letters weighing up to 200 grams until the end of 2002. Recently, however, the German government, citing slow postal reform by the European Commission, announced that it would delay the repeal of the postal monopoly until 2007.

Perhaps more important, Germany instituted meaningful changes in ownership structure. Deutsche Post purchased a 26 percent stake in DHL International, a leader in the global express industry, in 1998. Deutsche Post was partially privatized on November 20, 2000 in that country's largest public offering of the year. About 29 percent of the firm was offered publicly. The sale raised $5.6 billion. Investors applied for eight times the number of shares available.[14] Additionally the German government cleared the way for majority private ownership in Deutsche Post.[15] By all accounts Deutsche Post has become an aggressive competitor and has offered new products and services.

The Netherlands

The Netherlands is unique in that a majority of its postal service is now privately owned. The Dutch government transformed the post and telecommunications administration into Royal PTT Nederland (KPN) in 1989. PTT Post is the postal subsidiary of KPN. The Dutch government sold a 30 percent stake in KPN to the public in 1994 and another 22 percent stake in 1995 and thus reduced the government's share to 48 percent. The Ministry for Transportation and Public Works regulates PTT.

PTT Post retains a monopoly over the delivery of letters weighing up to 500 grams. Express mail services can compete in the reserved area as long as their prices are higher than PTT Post's. PTT Post faces a universal service obligation, which is funded through its monopoly service.

Unsurprisingly, privatization in the Netherlands created an aggressive, commercially oriented firm. PTT Post in 1991 joined with the post offices of France, Germany, the Netherlands, Canada, and Sweden to purchase 50 percent of the Australian transportation conglomerate TNT. In August 1996 PTT Post acquired complete control of the joint venture operations by purchasing TNT itself. In June 1998 KPN spun off TNT Post Group (TPG), which is now a fusion of a national post office and a global express company. TPG remains legally obligated to provide universal service and continues to enjoy a legal monopoly on the carriage of letters weighing 500 grams or less with specified price limits. TPG has announced its support for the repeal of its monopoly provided that other large competitors, such as Deutsche Post, are similarly stripped of monopoly protection.

Switzerland

Postal reform in Switzerland has not progressed as far as in some other European countries. The Swiss situation is similar to the U.S. case after passage of the Postal Reorganization Act of 1970. The Swiss case is instructive because Swiss postal reform was similar to U.S. reform and has produced similar results. The Swiss post historically was part of Swiss Post PTT, with both postal services and telecommunications. Postal services in Switzerland were organized by the Law on Postal Services of 1924 and the PTT (post and telecommunications) Organizational Law of 1960. Under those laws Swiss Post was a government-owned monopoly and was highly constrained in its business decisions. Like the U.S. Post Office, the government made postal pricing, financing, and personnel decisions. Politics dominated postal decisionmaking, and Swiss Post incurred large annual deficits.

Reform began in the early 1990s. In May 1992 the Swiss government passed a telecommunications law that liberalized some areas of that sector and eliminated the large subsidies of Swiss Post by Swiss Telecom as of January 1, 1998.[16] On December 31, 1997, Swiss PTT was split into two companies, Swiss Post and Swisscom. The Swiss Postal Law of 1998, however, was the key organizational reform with its five officially stated goals: (1) gradual liberalization of the postal market, (2) guaranteed universal service, (3) provision of financial means for universal service, (4) increased commercial freedom for Swiss Post, and (5) coping with EU developments in the postal sector.[17] At least some goals echo the intent of the Postal Reorganization Act of 1970. Similar to the Postal Reorganization Act, the Swiss Postal Law left Swiss Post as a government-owned monopoly and severely restricted it in terms of financing and personnel decisions. Swiss Post itself is required to provide universal service. Neither express mail nor international parcels fall under Swiss Post's monopoly, which is limited to mail and parcels up to 2 kilos. Money collected from monopolized activities finances universal service. There was also an attempt to imitate the board structure of a private corporation and to create a more "commercially oriented" atmosphere.

Several consequences of the Swiss law are similar to the U.S. experience. First, confusion exists over the degree to which competition laws apply to Swiss Post. Second, because Swiss Post remains government-owned, it continues to be constrained regarding capital and lacks sufficient cash to pursue meaningful research and development. It must go to the Swiss government, rather than to the capital markets, for additional capital. Third, controversy exists over the funding of pension liabilities, with negotiations underway between the government and Swiss Post about who will pay. Many personnel decisions remain in government hands. Wages are about 30 percent above market,[18] remarkably similar to the estimate of 28 percent for the USPS. Fourth, occasional political interventions occur, and decisionmaking processes are slow. Fifth, as in the United States, rates are set by contradictory norms.[19] An important difference between the Swiss and the U.S. laws is that the Swiss law, as per the suggestion of the European Union, limited the monopoly to provide just enough revenues to guarantee universal service.

Although an improvement over the old arrangements, the Swiss Postal Law reveals the same inadequacies as the Postal Reorganization Act. It underscores the importance of undertaking either meaningful ownership changes or increased competition.

Spain

Correos y Telegrafos is the government postal authority in Spain. Commercial freedoms were given to Correos in 1991. Correos bears examination because its monopoly power is defined in an unusual way. The reserved services in Spain are over the collection, distribution, and transportation of letters between cities and villages (interurban mail), while the delivery of letters within cities (intraurban mail) is open to competition. That situation is consistent with the original structure of postal services in the United States, which was to deliver mail between cities.[20] The scope of the postal monopoly was further reduced in 1997 to inter-urban services up to a maximum of five times the stamp price. There is no uniform rate in Spain: the price of mailing a letter depends on whether it is delivered to the same urban area or to another urban area within Spain.

United Kingdom

The Postal Services Act of 2000 radically altered postal services in the United Kingdom.[21] The act converted the British post office into Consignia, a private law company with all shares owned by the government. It also created a new regulator, the Postal Services Commission, or Postcomm.

The act created a detailed licensing scheme and abolished the postal monopoly. Postcomm was granted the exclusive authority to issue licenses, and no business may deliver letters without a license unless the price of delivery is at least £ 1 or the letter weighs at least 350 grams. Postcomm was given broad authority to grant licenses and to set conditions for licensees subject to the observance of three goals. First, Postcomm must ensure the provision of universal service. Service must be provided at uniform rates and must be affordable. Second, Postcomm must promote competition between postal operators. Third, Postcomm must "promote efficiency and economy on the part of the postal operators."[22] Postcomm may also place conditions on the services provided by a licensed operator outside of the reserved area.

Postcomm issued the first postal license to Consignia on March 23, 2001. The license set out detailed conditions regarding universal service obligations, service standards, prohibitions against unfair commercial advantage, and many other issues. Postcomm itself is able to define the meaning of the universal service obligation. It defines *universal service* as providing delivery service to each address each working day. In other countries the government defines it. Also the regulator must explicitly consider the effects on competition and efficiency when granting the license.

In January 2002 Postcomm proposed a three-stage process to eliminate the postal monopoly. The first phase, between April 2002 and March 2004, would eliminate the monopoly on bulk mail over 4,000 pieces per shipment and other services that amount to approximately 30 percent of Consignia's market.[23] Phase two, between April 2002 and March 2006, would likely eliminate the monopoly on another 30 percent of Consignia's market. Phase three, to take place no later than March 30, 2006, would end all restrictions on market entry.

The initial results of the UK reforms have not been positive. Consignia has recently sustained large losses, has cut 30,000 jobs, and will undergo further restructuring, including a name change.[24] Its privatized Dutch rival, TPG, has captured a substantial market share from Consignia. Commentators have suggested that Consignia's problems stem in part from its failure to privatize.[25]

Lessons from Global Reform

This overview of international postal reform provides several lessons. First, significant postal reform is possible and has taken place in numerous countries. Some postal services have welcomed reform while others have not. Despite some costs the preliminary evidence indicates that the net effect of reform has been positive.[26]

Second, to have meaningful effects, postal reform must include changes in market structure, through clear limitations on or elimination of the postal monopoly, or changes in ownership, through the issuance of ownership shares. A minor alteration in organizational or regulatory structures, absent one or both of those more fundamental reforms, is unlikely to have significant effects on performance.

Third, the universal service obligation must be made a responsibility of government, rather than of the postal operator. The government would thus gain vital flexibility in its approach to ensuring rural delivery and in defining universal service.[27] Fourth, when changes in ownership or added commercial flexibility are introduced, it is critical that rigorous antitrust oversight be applied to the new entity. Government-owned firms, or firms that were previously government-owned, often retain various special privileges. Their special status may give them an artificial competitive advantage, which can be exploited. I have attempted to incorporate these lessons in my suggestions for postal reform in the United States.

7

A Proposal for Postal Reform

Debate on the process of postal reform in the United States has suffered from a confusion of two distinct issues: issues of market structure (government-enforced monopoly versus competition) and issues of ownership (the creation of well-defined, transferable residual claims). It is crucial to separate those issues so that reform can proceed.

Some commentators have inferred that the creation of residual claims implies an abandonment of universal delivery. That is clearly not the case, as the international experience indicates. Moreover, many privately owned firms in the United States, such as electric and water utilities, confront a universal service mandate within their monopoly service areas.

Creating Transferable Ownership Shares

The residual claims of the USPS are poorly defined and are not transferable. The creation of well-defined, transferable claims would yield large social benefits. Resistance to the creation of such claims is likely to come from two politically influential groups: postal employees and rural customers. Managers and postal workers are the de facto residual claimants of the Postal Service, but they cannot transfer those claims. They receive part of the residual by absorbing higher revenues through increased wages. Employees have the political power to significantly affect reform. Therefore, to ensure the political feasibility of postal reform, it must be in employees' interest.

The second group, rural customers, fear any change in market structure that is perceived as threatening rural service. Members of

Congress rationally respond to those fears by opposing reform. The initial reform efforts must focus on the creation of transferable ownership shares and the appropriate regulatory structures to accompany that change, rather than on the elimination of the postal monopoly. Once fundamental changes in ownership structure are in place, questions of market structure, divorced from contentious property rights issues, can be cast in a clearer light.

A first step in the reform process is thus to state clearly that the government would continue to guarantee nationwide delivery of letter mail at uniform rates. As in Germany and Sweden, however, guaranteeing universal service would become the responsibility of the federal government, rather than of the USPS per se. The USPS would thus be freed of its responsibility to provide universal service. As the discussion of reform in other countries suggests, that key step would give the government greater flexibility in providing and defining universal service. It would eliminate the need to pay for universal service through markups on urban delivery, and remove the putative motive for government-owned monopoly. It would also emphasize that the initial phase of the reform debate would focus on ownership rather than on the adequacy of rural delivery. All questions of isolated rural customers, the dangers of cream-skimming entry, etc., would become irrelevant because the federal government would continue to guarantee rural service.

The second step would issue transferable residual claims in the USPS, as in Germany and Holland. The creation of transferable residual claims is critical for improvements in corporate governance as well as for changes in firm objectives and incentives. The USPS would be unlikely to alter its incentives meaningfully, and thus its previous patterns of performance, without a significant change in ownership structure.

The creation of private ownership in the Postal Service would likely have a greater effect on performance than any other single reform. Transferable ownership would create a market for postal shares and determine a price for those shares. It would allow the use of the numerous incentive mechanisms discussed above, including stock options and bonuses based on stock returns. Managers in particular could be granted stock options, restricted stock, and performance-based incentives. Such a stock offering would raise much-needed capital that could be used for modernization.

The firm would also be subject to typical financial market checks, such as regular audits, SEC reporting requirements, and examinations by bond-rating and investors' services. The experience in other countries and other industries indicates that firms with private owners would behave as profit-maximizers and would likely become efficient, vigorous competitors.

The Net Value of the Postal Service. Before privatization all USPS assets should be inventoried and evaluated at market prices. The list to be inventoried must include all valuable property owned by the USPS, including land, buildings, service locations, leasehold property, easement options, mineral reserves, water, forestry land and timber, and operational property, such as power stations, warehouses, machinery, mobile equipment, and rolling stock. Fixed assets, such as land, buildings, machinery, equipment, and vehicles, are usually evaluated on the balance sheet at historical cost. Historical cost tends to understate the value of certain assets, such as downtown post offices. Estimates suggest that the assets of the USPS are worth several times their reported value.[1]

Evidence indicates that the liabilities of the USPS are substantially underreported as well for two main reasons. First, the USPS treats its deferred retirement costs, which are currently about $33 billion (or more than half its assets), as a "regulatory asset." According to generally accepted accounting principles (GAAP), a regulated firm can consider a deferred cost to be an asset if those costs are likely to be recovered through higher rates in the future.[2] It is conceivable that, in 1970, the demand for letter delivery was sufficiently inelastic to allow future recovery of retirement costs through rates, but the technological changes already discussed, and the rapid growth in retirement costs, make that prospect unlikely today.

Second, the USPS does not report the liability for its long-term retiree health benefits, or its long-term liability for retiree pension cost of living increases, on its balance sheet.[3] The costs of health benefits are expensed as they occur. Alan Robinson and David Rawnsley calculated that depending on the discount rate used, the Postal Service's current liability for its retiree health care costs is $28–47 billion.[4] Given its substantial underused and underreported assets, coupled with its off-balance-sheet liabilities, it is difficult to calculate the true current net value of the USPS. The former PMG Henderson, however, estimated that value at $65–100 billion.[5]

Arguments that the USPS cannot be privately owned because it has negative net worth are specious, however. The organizational structure of the USPS is a creature of government. Congress can assume USPS liabilities to the degree it desires and thus create a valuable organization. The value of the USPS is endogenous to the details of reorganization.[6]

Employee Ownership. The third element of reform is to ensure that postal employees have a stake in the reform process. Although U.S. taxpayers are the legal owners of the Postal Service, and thus have rights to its value, postal employees' de facto political rights must be taken into account.[7] Employees are unlikely to give up their rights without compensation. Additionally, employees have built their careers on a government-created post, and reform would likely disrupt those careers. It thus seems appropriate that some compensation be offered when mandating a shift from government to private ownership.

Employees could be given a stake in reform in several ways. First, the government should stress that it would guarantee workers' pension and retirement funds. That would be a key element in gaining employee support. Next, employees should be offered shares in the Postal Service at a discount from market price, assuming they would be willing to retain those shares for a specified period. Given a sufficient discount, many employees would likely accept such an offer. Essentially a transfer from taxpayer-owners to USPS employees, that offer would have important benefits beyond mere political expedience. If employees were required to remain owners for a certain period, they would develop a sense of connection to the larger organization. Ownership would improve employees' incentives and make them more cost-conscious and more willing to operate the USPS efficiently. Employees would likely bring fewer grievances if they had an ownership stake in the organization.[8] It would also change the general culture and atmosphere at the USPS. Postmaster General Henderson called for privatization of the USPS and suggested an employee stock ownership plan:

> Postal employees would benefit most and would work hardest if they owned the company, in much the same way that employees of Delta Airlines own theirs. In an employee-owned postal company, raises would be based on stock value. And as the company grew in value, employee wealth would grow as well.[9]

Such an ownership change would be in the public interest and would be politically feasible if properly structured, but it would require an important concurrent modification of existing regulatory structures.

Appropriate Regulatory and Institutional Structures

The creation of tradable ownership shares in the Postal Service would create an organizational form that is much more familiar in the United States: a privately owned firm with at least one type of legally monopolized service. Questions regarding a wide variety of issues, including the setting of wages, the setting of rates, the appointment of board members, the right to strike, and other labor relations issues (including collective bargaining with binding arbitration), could be answered by reference to the regulation of privately owned firms. The lessons from regulating (and deregulating) electricity, gas, airlines, trucking, and numerous other industries could then be applied to postal services.

Powers of the Postal Rate Commission. As a direct consequence of private ownership, the powers of the Postal Rate Commission would have to be increased to reflect more closely those of a typical state public utility commission. My proposal envisions an increase in the commission's power in several ways. The commission currently has staff members who are experts in postal law and economics. It could easily add to that other experts as needed to undertake additional responsibilities. It is the most logical body to undertake those responsibilities.

Rate-setting authority. First, the Postal Rate Commission should be given the actual authority to set rates, or to set caps on rates, for individual mail classes. The board of governors' authority to overturn the decisions of the commission should be repealed.[10] That action would provide the commission with additional power to control subsidies across classes of mail, which would likely become even more of a concern under private ownership.[11]

Under private ownership the power of the commission would, in another way, increase automatically. With the existence of transferable residual claims and with enhanced rate-setting authority, the commission could reduce equity values through unfavorable rate decisions. Rate decisions would then directly affect all variables tied to equity values, including stockholder wealth and senior management pay. The commission's power would thus increase directly as a result of private ownership itself.

Once ownership shares were created, the appropriate regulatory regime could be implemented. Price cap regulation might be a desirable regime. Price caps set rates through an index, typically some measure of inflation minus an X-factor that accounts for productivity improvement.[12] A firm is allowed to retain any profits earned under a price cap. Because a firm can retain the residual, it has the incentive to innovate and to operate efficiently.

Although price cap regulation has much to recommend it, its effectiveness depends crucially on the existence of tradable residual claims.[13] Without well-defined residual claimants, a firm has no incentive to maximize profit subject to the price cap and thus no incentive to minimize costs. A move to price cap regulation should therefore be viewed not as an isolated reform, but only as a complement to the creation of tradable residual claims. If the USPS obtained more interproduct price discretion under price caps, however, then the ability of the commission to constrain cross-subsidization might weaken. Price caps must be implemented with care.

The commission should also acquire various other powers typically held by state public utility commissions. Examples include the statutory authority to subpoena information, and the ability to regulate the quality of postal services directly, including the frequency and speed of deliveries.

Licensing authority. As noted, Congress, rather than the Postal Service itself, must assume responsibility for guaranteeing universal mail service. Because that involves highly specialized knowledge, a natural step would be for Congress to delegate responsibility for ensuring universal service to the Postal Rate Commission. The commission could then use a licensing scheme to ensure universal service. Here reforms in other countries are instructive, as Germany, Sweden, Norway, and the United Kingdom have implemented licensing systems. Licenses should be granted under the condition that the licensee provide universal delivery and particular levels of service, etc. The commission may wish to contract with the USPS to provide universal service in some areas. Because the USPS itself contracts out delivery in some rural areas, however, the commission might wish to license those delivery companies directly. Licenses should be renegotiated at particular intervals, and service standards would have to be maintained to ensure relicensing.

Moreover, the license should include detailed requirements regarding rates, service standards, and other aspects of postal operations. For example, when Postcomm issued the first postal license in the United Kingdom to Consignia on March 23, 2001, it was highly detailed:

> Twenty conditions are attached, addressing issues such as prices, universal service obligations, standards of service, complaint handling, free services for the blind, provision of information to users, integrity of mail, access to postal facilities, prohibitions against unfair commercial advantage, mergers, accounting rules, financial resources, and reports to Postcomm. The universal service obligations set out in the Consignia license are detailed. For example, Consignia must make delivery to each address point at least once each working day. It must establish collection boxes so that "in each postcode area where the delivery point density is not less than 200 delivery points per square kilometres not less than 99% of users or

potential users of postal services are within 500 meters of a post office letter box."[14]

The Postal Rate Commission could carefully regulate all aspects of postal services through such a mechanism. It would have the authority to ensure that universal delivery was provided and that service standards were maintained.[15] It could implement price caps because of its licensing power. Additionally the commission could address issues such as the elimination of the mailbox monopoly through a licensing scheme. The commission should retain the authority to license postal operators so that customers could gain confidence in the ability of a new ownership regime to ensure universal service.

Additional Commercial Flexibility. Along with creation of private ownership, the Postal Service should be given additional commercial freedom. Subject to the terms of its license, the Postal Service should be allowed to close unprofitable post offices or replace them with contract service. This step requires changing section 101(b) of the Postal Reorganization Act, which prohibits the closure of post offices.

The privatized USPS could also divest itself of certain activities and could make acquisitions, again subject to the terms of its license. The sale of numerous underperforming properties at market prices would raise the value of the USPS.[16] It might wish to divest its package delivery system. It could also sell valuable downtown properties and move sorting centers to less costly locations and thus more efficiently allocate resources and realize the latent value of those properties.[17] Some sorting centers were established when mail was moved by rail and are consequently located near the nexus of rail lines in central business areas. With the majority of mail now moved by truck, those sorting centers could be more efficiently located in less populated locations. Under the current system, without a profit motive, it is difficult to know which activities are economically justified. To improve its economic viability, a privately owned firm would likely make a wide variety of adjustments, which are difficult to predict ex ante. In general, privatization would give the USPS the incentive to maintain the proper scale and scope for its activities.

Avoiding Special Privileges. As the experience with postal reform in other countries suggests, it is critical that a privately owned postal service not retain various quasi-governmental powers, privileges, and immunities that could result in large implicit subsidies and thus seriously distort market behavior. For example, it would be undesirable if lenders were to treat debt securities issued by the new entity as possessing an implicit federal guarantee against default, as that would distort the price of its debt and result in a hidden subsidy.

A key challenge for reform is thus to structure the new enterprise at the onset so that investors will not anticipate government support. Eliminating special privileges held by the USPS, including the right to borrow from the Treasury, the exemption from SEC reporting requirements, and the right of eminent domain, could facilitate such a structure. Moreover, antitrust laws should apply to a privatized firm. The firm would no longer be protected from antitrust prosecution on the grounds of sovereign immunity. Strict antitrust enforcement would supplement the actions of the Postal Rate Commission and would signal that the government was serious about avoiding special privileges.

Changes in Market Structure

Delivery service, like trucking, is an inherently competitive industry. The social gains from introducing competition are likely to be substantial.[18] The final step in the reform process is therefore to introduce complete competition into the market for postal services, as in Sweden, Finland, and New Zealand.

The appropriate long-term structure for postal services is a fully competitive market, that is, free entry at all service levels. Competition could be introduced gradually through reductions in the reserved area of service. Introducing competition slowly would have both benefits and costs. Gradual reductions in the postal monopoly might be the only way that competition could be made politically palatable. Rural customers might fear inadequate mail service if the monopoly were repealed and competition were introduced suddenly.

Measured reductions in the monopoly would allow new firms to enter over time and would build confidence in the market's ability to provide delivery services. That process would help diffuse rural customers' concerns about further deregulation, which would in turn reduce the pressure from members of Congress to stall further competition. Second, the gradual introduction of competition would allow the dominant firm to adjust its pricing, labor force, capital stock, and product array.

The main cost of introducing competition slowly is the risk of halting further reform. As in Germany, the legislature could delay the introduction of complete competition. If the new postal operator were privately owned, it might defend its monopoly power even more vigorously because the monopoly would then have greater value. Such risks, however, must be accepted to make postal reform possible.

Much as the Civil Aeronautics Board was abolished after the deregulation of airlines, the final step in reforming postal services in the United States would be the abolition of the Postal Rate Commission. With privatization of the USPS and the introduction of full competition, market forces would fully regulate postal services. Commission regulation would be unnecessary. market forces would indeed provide more effective checks on firm behavior than regulatory constraints presently provide. Competition in product markets would ensure efficient, comprehensive service. Stock and bond markets, through takeovers, price signals, incentive pay, removals, bond ratings, investor services, and a variety of other mechanisms, would continuously monitor and constrain the behavior of managers. Postal services would become an efficient, customer-oriented industry.

Summary

The traditional structure for postal services worldwide, a fully vertically integrated government-owned firm with a legally enforced monopoly over letter delivery, is ill-suited for the modern competitive communications marketplace. Further technological change will only exacerbate that mismatch. Postal services internationally have suffered from the increasing availability of alternative methods of communications. Many countries have confronted those concerns by significantly reforming their postal services. The preliminary evidence indicates that reform has positive effects.

Significant postal reform in the United States is inevitable. The Postal Service's losses are likely to grow. Additional rate increases will only accelerate substitution into alternative ways of communicating, while the price of those alternatives is falling. The Postal Service will not remain viable in its present form without a return to large direct taxpayer subsidies. Part of the motivation for passing the Postal Reorganization Act of 1970 was to eliminate such subsidies and make the Postal Service financially self-sufficient.

For the wide variety of reasons indicated, the most appropriate institutional structure for postal services is an industry featuring free entry and offering tradable residual claims, or transferable property rights to the net cash flows of the organization. Such a structure is in the public interest and would better achieve the goals of the 1970 act.

My proposal advocates the creation of transferable residual claims in the Postal Service as a first step in reform. In conjunction with that step, the Postal Rate Commission must be given substantial additional authority to control rates, universal service standards, potential anticompetitive behavior, and many other aspects of postal services. I suggest that the commission be authorized to use a licensing scheme to effectuate that control. A number of additional reforms would stem from the creation of residual claims, including additional commercial flexibility for the Postal Service, while eliminating its special privileges.

After the establishment of tradable ownership shares, the postal monopoly could be eliminated. The reserved area of service could be gradually reduced so that competition would be permitted in successively larger segments of the letter delivery market. That reform would build confidence in the ability of the market to provide letter delivery.

8

Summary and Conclusions

The U.S. Post Office experienced severe operational and financial turmoil in the mid-1960s. Its deficits were rapidly increasing, its labor force was demoralized, its productivity was low, and its infrastructure was antiquated. It could not handle rising quantities of mail. Congress responded by passing the Postal Reorganization Act of 1970. The modifications embodied in the act were more sweeping than any others in the U.S. postal system's long history and were among the most extensive ever for a federal agency.

Through the act Congress hoped to increase postal productivity, to make the Post Office more businesslike, to reduce its reliance on government subsidies, and to place more of the cost of mail delivery on mail users by making the Postal Service self-financing. It also hoped to rationalize the postal rate structure, to improve labor relations and working conditions, and to make the postal system less subject to political influence.

On some counts the act achieved its goals. Postal productivity improved, direct subsidies from the Treasury decreased, and direct congressional control over the postal function diminished. Mail users now pay more of the cost of mail delivery. The act, however, failed on several essential counts. The rationality of the rate structure, as measured by the degree of cross-subsidy from competitive to monopolistic mail classes, apparently worsened. Although postal productivity is higher, those improvements were not passed on to customers in the form of more pieces delivered per dollar spent. The Postal Service has not been successful in protecting the taxpayer's initial equity investment, which has dissipated over time. Postal wages have not been maintained at levels comparable to those in private industry as mandated by the act. Finally,

128

the act has not eliminated political influence over the Postal Service but has merely changed its form. The act failed to achieve all its goals because it eliminated direct control over the postal function through Congress but did not replace that control with market constraints either through product market competition or through the numerous market-based controls facing privately owned and publicly traded corporations.

Further reform of the U.S. Postal Service is timely. The Postal Service is losing substantial amounts of money, while rates are rising rapidly. Unlike the situation in 1970, alternative methods of communicating, such as telephones, facsimiles, and electronic mail, are today widespread. Rate increases will cause consumers to substitute into those alternatives and further reduce the Postal Service's market share. The long-term outlook for the Postal Service, at least in its current form, is bleak.

Rather than thwarting the original goals of reorganization, further reform would instead help achieve them. Debate on the process of postal reform in the United States has suffered from a confusion of two distinct issues: issues of market structure (government-enforced monopoly compared with competition) and issues of ownership (the creation of well-defined, transferable residual claims). It is crucial to separate those issues so that reform can proceed. Chapter 7 outlined how tradable residual claims can be created while the Postal Service temporarily retains a monopoly over delivery.

The creation of tradable residual claims would improve postal performance for at least four reasons. First, it would greatly enhance corporate governance, as discussed in chapter 5. Second, it would provide the Postal Service with incentives to minimize costs, which would result in the adoption of a host of efficiency-improving measures. Third, it would convert the Postal Service into an organizational form that is more familiar in the United States: a privately owned, regulated firm enjoying restricted entry. That organizational form is similar to that of industries that were de-monopolized in the 1970s and 1980s.

Fourth, the creation of residual claims would establish clear firm objectives, which are now lacking. Currently, powerful special interests can exploit the Postal Service's lack of direction and use its monopoly power for their own benefit. In terms of the act's specific goals, the creation of tradable residual claims would end equity depletion, help the Postal Service to break even (and instead to earn profits), and greatly improve managerial efficiency by subjecting managers to a variety of control mechanisms.

Significant regulatory change must accompany the creation of tradable residual claims. The universal service obligation must be a responsibility of the federal government, not of the Postal Service. The Postal Rate Commission must be given substantial additional power to control the Postal Service, or it will become a weakly regulated, privately owned firm with government-enforced monopoly power. The commission should acquire the authority to grant detailed licenses to postal operators, as in the United Kingdom. Through its licensing authority the commission can control rates, quality of service, the degree of competition, and many other variables. It can restrict the postal monopoly by limiting it to specified multiples of the stamp price.

The Postal Service must also be granted additional commercial flexibility, such as the authority to close post offices (keeping in mind the government's responsibility to provide universal service). It should also be deprived of all special privileges and immunities, such as subsidized borrowing, powers of eminent domain, and immunity from antitrust prosecution.

Once those critical institutional reforms are in place, the Postal Rate Commission can gradually reduce the scope of the Postal Service's monopoly by contracting the size of the reserved area. The contraction would allow competition to be introduced steadily but slowly and thus build confidence in the market's ability to provide delivery of letter mail.

Meaningful postal reform is feasible and has been accomplished in other countries. The postal services of Germany and Holland are now privately owned. Full market competition has been introduced in Finland, Sweden, and New Zealand. Through limitations on the reserved area of service, increased competition has been introduced in a variety of countries. The citizens of those countries are beginning to enjoy the benefits of vigorous postal reform, and Americans may soon do the same.

Appendix A

Description of Data Sources

1. **Price Index Data.** The price index for 1930 to 1997 was constructed from two sources. First, table B-3: Implicit price deflators for gross domestic product, 1959–1994, from *The Economic Report of the President* (1995, 278) was used. Second, for data before 1959, the table Series F 1-5, "Gross National Product, Total and Per Capita, in Current and 1958 Prices: 1869 to 1970" (which provides an implicit price index) from the *Historical Statistics of the United States*, Department of Commerce, was used. The base year used, as in table B-3, was 1987. *The Economic Report of the President* (1998) was used for later years.

2. **Population Data.** Data on U.S. population for the years 1930–1970 were obtained from the *Historical Statistics of the United States*, Department of Commerce, series A 29-42, "Annual Estimates of the Population, by Age: 1900–1970" (10). For years after 1970 the data were obtained from *The Economic Report of the President.*

3. **Nonpostal Wages.** For wages in government, services, manufacturing, communications, and utilities, the data source for 1930–1988 was the *National Income and Product Accounts of the United States,* volumes 1 and 2. In each case the table "Wages and Salaries per Full-Time Equivalent Employee by Industry" was used. For years after 1988, the data were obtained from the *Survey of Current Business,* various issues.

4. **Postal Wages.** Data on the total salary bill of postal workers were obtained from *The Annual Report of the Postmaster General* for the years 1930–1967. For years after 1967, the data were obtained from the United States Postal Service report, "Postal Service National Payroll Hours Summary Reports" (consolidated).

5. **Total Factor Productivity Data.** Data on USPS total factor productivity were obtained from *United States Postal Service Annual Total Factor Productivity: 1992 Annual Tables* published by Christensen Associates (December 1992). The data are presented in table 8-6, "Workload, Input and Total Factor Productivity" (1972=1.0).

Appendix B

Description of the Major Mail Classes

All descriptions of mail classes are from George S. Tolley, "Direct Testimony of George S. Tolley on Behalf of the United States Postal Service," testimony before the Postal Rate Commission, Postal Rate and Fee Changes, 1994, Docket R94-1.

First-Class Mail

The most distinguishing feature of First-Class Mail is that is contains private messages. Handwritten or typewritten message, as well as hard-copy computer output if it has the character of personal correspondence, must be sent by First-Class Mail. Bills, statements of account and messages associated with a business transaction are considered to be private messages and must be sent by First-Class Mail. (Tolley, p. 24).

Second-Class Mail

Second-class mail consists of newspapers, magazines, and other periodicals. Nearly all second-class mail originates in the non-household sector. . . Second-class mail is used solely by the publishers and registered agents of newspapers, magazines, and other periodical publications which meet the qualifications of the Domestic Mail Manual. To qualify for second-class rates the material to be mailed must be printed and issued regularly (at least four times per year). Second-class material is published for the purpose of disseminating information of a public character, such as news, or is devoted to literature, the sciences, arts, or some special industry. (Tolley, p. 101)

Third-Class Mail

Third-class mail is mostly printed advertising, solicitation, and promotional materials and also small parcels. Third-class includes matter not required to be mailed First-Class, and is subject to postal inspection. All third-class mail must weigh less than 16 ounces (*Domestic Mail Manual,* issue 46, C300.1.1).

Printed advertisements sent as third-class mail come in a wide variety of forms, from single page advertising circulars to multi-page color catalogs. Businesses, running from the very small to the extremely large, are the primary senders of third-class mail. (Tolley, p.134)

Fourth-Class Mail

Fourth-class mail is a less expensive alternative for sending eligible mail pieces weighing between one and 70 pounds that are not sent as Priority Mail and are not accepted under second-class restrictions. In general, fourth-class mail tends to contain tangible objects (e.g., merchandise, household items) rather than correspondence. . . . The four subclasses in fourth-class mail are: parcel post, bound printed matter, special rate, and library rate. (Tolley, p. 185)

Notes

Chapter 1: Introduction

1. U.S. Postal Service, *2001 Annual Report* (Washington, D.C.: USPS, 2001).

2. U.S. Postal Service, *Transformation Plan* (Washington, D.C.: USPS, 2002), p. i.

3. U.S. Department of Commerce, Economics and Statistics Administration, *Statistical Abstract of the United States 2000* (Washington, D.C.: Government Printing Office, 2002), t 669, pp. 416–18, and t 684, p. 428.

4. The President's Commission on Postal Reorganization, *Toward Postal Excellence* (Washington, D.C.: Government Printing Office, 1968), p. 13.

5. Ibid., p. 11.

6. Public Law 91-375, 84 Stat. 719, 39 U.S.C. 101 et. seq. The act became effective on July 1, 1971.

7. Scholars in political science have recognized the act's historic importance. See, for example, John T. Tierney, *Postal Reorganization: Managing the Public's Business* (Boston: Auburn House, 1981), p. xv: "Save for the creation of the Department of Defense in 1949, it is difficult to think of other changes in the executive branch of government that have been more comprehensive."

8. For exceptions see Donald R. Ewing and Roger K. Salaman, *The Postal Crisis: The Postal Function as a Communications Service* (Washington, D.C.: U.S. Department of Commerce, Office of Telecommunications, 1977), and R. Richard Geddes, "The Economic Effects of Postal Reorganization," *Journal of Regulatory Economics* 13 (1998): 139.

9. Indeed the USPS announced that it would lose $1.68 billion in the fiscal year ending September 30, 2001, according to "Postal Service Cites Terrorism, Economy in $1.68 Billion Loss," in the December 5, 2001, *Baltimore Sun.* Even with stamp prices rising to 37 cents, the Postal Service expects to lose $2 billion in its 2002 fiscal year, according to "Postal Panel Set to Increase Rates; First-Class Stamp Will Rise to 37 Cents," in the March 22, 2002, *Wall Street Journal.*

10. U.S. General Accounting Office, *U.S. Postal Service: Deteriorating Financial Outlook Increases Need for Transformation* (Washington, D.C.: 2002)

11. See Clifford Winston, "Economic Deregulation: Days of Reckoning for Microeconomists," *Journal of Economic Literature* 31 (September 1993): 1263–89, for an excellent summary of the details of regulatory reform in each industry and its effects. For a more recent assessment of deregulation in airlines, railroads, telecommunications, and electricity, see Sam Peltzman and Clifford Winston, *Deregulation of Network Industries: What's Next?* (Washington, D.C.: AEI-Brookings Joint Center for Regulatory Studies, 2000).

12. Germany originally planned to abolish its monopoly in 2002, but the German Parliament approved a law extending the letter monopoly until 2007 due to the slow pace of European Union reform. See *Financial Times*, Eur. ed., June 29, 2001, p. 3.

13. "Shares Rose 2.4% on Debut Day for Deutsche Post," *New York Times*, Nov. 21, 2000.

14. "Path Clear for Sale of Deutsche Post," *Financial Times*, U.S. ed., July 26, 2001.

15. *Toward Postal Excellence*, p. 2.

Chapter 2: The Post Office and the Reorganization Act

1. John T. Tierney, *The U.S. Postal Service: Status and Prospects of a Public Enterprise* (Boston: Auburn House, 1988), p. 10.

2. John T.Tierney, *Postal Reorganization: Managing the Public's Business* (Boston: Auburn House, 1981), p. 105–6

3. *Wall Street Journal,* September 20, 1967, p. 3.

4. "New Era Favors Career Postmasters," *Postal Life,* May 1969, pp. 8–11. See also President's Commission on Postal Reorganization, *Toward Postal Excellence*, p. 41.

5. *Toward Postal Excellence*, annex, vol. 4, pt. 7, p. 44. See also George L. Priest, "Socialism, Eastern Europe, and the Question of the Postal Monopoly," in *Governing the Postal Service,* edited by J. Gregory Sidak (Washington, D.C.: AEI Press, 1994), p. 51, on high postal unionization rates.

6. Richard F. Fenno, *Congressmen in Committees* (Boston: Little Brown, 1973), p. 246.

7. Ibid.

8. *Toward Postal Excellence*, p. 33.

9. Ibid., p. 28, states: "Management has little pertinent financial information on the costs of postal activities. The members of the Commission found it hard to believe that a postmaster sees no information on the total costs of his operations."

10. See Tierney, *Postal Reorganization,* p. 8. By rents I mean rates of return above the competitive level.

11. Additionally, because labor votes but capital does not, political benefits obtain from maintaining a labor-intensive technology.

12. Tierney, *U.S. Postal Service*, p. 12.
13. *Toward Postal Excellence*, p. 12.
14. Tierney, *Postal Reorganization*, pp. 15–16.
15. "Study 5: Postal Rate-Making," in *Toward Postal Excellence*, pp. 145–53.

Chapter 3: The Organization of the U.S. Postal Service

1. Donald R. Ewing and Roger K. Salaman, *The Postal Crisis: The Postal Function as a Communications Service* (Washington, D.C.: U.S. Department of Commerce, Office of Telecommunications, 1977), p. 25.
2. Joel L. Fleishman, *The Future of the Postal Service* (New York: Praeger, 1983), p. 63.
3. Public Law 94-421, 90 Stat. 1303 (1976) (codified at 39 U.S.C. § 2401 (d)) (1976). See S. Rep. 966, 94th Cong., 2d Sess. (1976), U.S. Code Cong. and Admin. News, 1976, at 2400.
4. 39 U.S.C. § 3624 (c)(1).
5. 39 U.S.C. § 3625 (a).
6. Cited in James I. Campbell Jr. "An Introduction to the History of the Postal Monopoly Law in the United States," mimeo, revised June 27, 1995; available at http://www.jcampbell.com. See also George L. Priest, "The History of the Postal Monopoly in the United States," *Journal of Law and Economics* 18 (1975): 80, for a discussion of the history of the postal monopoly in the United States.
7. The USPS instituted a new mail classification system in July 1996. First-class mail includes personal correspondence, post cards, and business transactions. Standard mail A, formerly called third-class mail, includes letters and flats. Advertisers mailing identical pieces in bulk use this class of mail. For a more complete description of the new mail classes, see USPS, *1996 Annual Report*, pp. 39–40 and appendix. For a detailed discussion of the extent of the postal monopoly, see chapter 2 in J. Gregory Sidak and Daniel F. Spulber, *Protecting Competition from the Postal Monopoly* (Washington, D.C.: AEI Press, 1996). The monopoly power is a frequent topic of policy discussion. See, for example, Douglas K. Adie, *Monopoly Mail: Privatizing the U.S. Postal Service* (New York: Transaction, 1989); Peter J. Ferrara, *Free the Mail: Ending the Postal Monopoly* (Washington, D.C.: Cato Institute, 1990); Edward L. Hudgins, *The Last Monopoly: Privatizing the Postal Service for the Information Age* (Washington, D.C.: Cato Institute, 1996); and James C. Miller III, "End the Postal Monopoly," *Cato Journal* 5 (1985): 149.
8. 39 C.F.R. § 310.1(a). Sidak and Spulber, *Protecting Competition*, p. 12, also note the phenomenon: "The result is unlike that in any other regulated industry: Because the Postal Service claims for itself the term 'letter,' which defines the extent of its monopoly, the monopolist has the power largely to define the scope of its own monopoly." According to the Postal Service's definition, an addressed grocery store advertisement is a letter. The courts have

accepted the Postal Service's broad test for a letter as "the presence or absence of an address." *Associated Third Class Mail Users v. United States Postal Service,* 600 F.2d 824, (830 D.C. Cir. 1979) (Wright, J.).

9. See James I. Campbell Jr., "Postal Monopoly Law," p. 18. Campbell documents how the Post Office and then the Postal Service has systematically expanded the scope of its monopoly over 200 years.

10. Ibid., pp. 18–19:

> In 1974, the Postal Service adopted comprehensive monopoly regulations that substantially revised the previous administrative definition of *letter* to read "a message in or on a physical object sent to a specific address." This definition manifestly included within the postal monopoly all physical communications, whether recorded by means of writing, printing, photography, or electromagnetic process.

11. See President's Commission on Postal Reorganization, *Toward Postal Excellence,* pp. 128–29. Those remain the most frequently cited justifications, though perhaps not the most compelling.

12. Postal Reorganization Act, sect. 7 (1970).

13. Priest, "History of the Postal Monopoly," p. 69.

14. 18 U.S.C §1725.

15. *Domestic Mail Manual* § 151.2. Clearly the monopoly is designed to preserve revenues.

16. Robert H. Cohen, William W. Ferguson, John D. Waller, and Spyros S. Xenakis, "An Analysis of the Potential for Cream Skimming in the U.S. Residential Delivery Market," in *Emerging Competition in Postal and Delivery Services,* edited by Michael A. Crew and Paul R. Kleindorfer (Amsterdam: Kluwer Academic Publishers, 1999), p. 143n12.

17. 453 U.S. (1981) at 128. See Sidak and Spulber, *Protecting Competition,* pp. 35–37, for a discussion of this case.

18. Sidak and Spulber, *Protecting Competition,* pp. 37–38.

19. Discouraging such competition was the original reason for the creation of the mailbox monopoly in 1936. See ibid., p. 34–35.

20. See Priest, "History of the Postal Monopoly," p. 52.

21. The details of this justification have changed considerably over time. *Postal service,* referring to the delivery of mail utilizing a series of posts along post roads housing men and horses, was naturally an intercity service. Customers could drop off letters—called *drop letters*—for delivery in the same city. As late as 1863 the Post Office considered that service to be secondary. Private delivery of drop letters was legal, and by one count 147 private local postal companies operated in the mid-nineteenth century. See Campbell, "Postal Monopoly Law," p. 14. The Post Office did not gain a monopoly over

local delivery until the Act of March 3, 1872, a comprehensive revision of the postal code. The Postal Service later argued that revenues from serving dense urban routes had to be maintained to subsidize sparse rural routes. Thus it utilized the 1872 expansion of its monopoly power to justify the retention of its monopoly 100 years later.

22. Priest, "History of the Postal Monopoly," p. 66. The argument is unappealing, however, because private expresses, including the Pony Express, were already serving rural routes.

23. The cross-subsidy or universal service justification is not the historical reason for postal monopolies. In Colonial America as in many other countries, the monarch monopolized postal delivery to ensure secure military communications and to catch spies more easily. Postal delivery came to be viewed as a public service, with the government having a duty to provide universal delivery in exchange for its monopoly power. Over time those two issues became convoluted, and the justification became that to satisfy its universal service obligation, the post had to retain a monopoly to avoid the deleterious effects of cream skimming. See David Rawnsley and Nomi Lazar, "Managing the Universal Service Obligation," in *Emerging Competition in Postal and Delivery Services*, edited by Michael A. Crew and Paul R. Kleindorfer (Amsterdam: Kluwer Academic Publishers, 1999), p. 184: "It is safe to conclude that historically we do not have postal monopolies in order to provide for universal service."

24. U.S. Postal Service, *Statutes Restricting Private Carriage of Mail and Their Administration* 11-13, 68, 186 (House Committee on Post Office and Civil Service, 93rd Cong., 1st sess., comm. print 1973). The cream-skimming argument also appears in *Toward Postal Excellence*, p. 129. Priest, "History of the Postal Monopoly," p. 69, states, "The Congress in 1970 was not unaware that the chief justification for the monopoly has been to protect the cross-subsidization of rural delivery."

25. *Washington Post*, September 23, 1996, p. A17.

26. Tierney, *U.S. Postal Service*, p. 32.

27. Differences in delivery costs between densely and sparsely populated areas also likely existed in early America, where delivery by horse or on foot was used to provide intercity service. Transport costs were a large portion of total delivery costs and necessarily imply that delivery to a distant city is more costly than to one nearby.

28. Robert H. Cohen, William W. Ferguson, and Spyros S. Xenakis, "Rural Delivery and the Universal Service Obligation," in *Regulation and the Nature of Postal and Delivery Services,* edited by Michael A. Crew and Paul R. Kleindorfer (Amsterdam: Kluwer Academic Publishers, 1993), p. 161. About 25 percent of the U.S. population lives in rural areas.

29. The Postal Service has never empirically demonstrated that urban-rural cost differentials are significant. In appendix F II to the 1973 Board of Governors' report, prepared by McKinsey and Company, it was estimated

that, under the worst of circumstances, competition would result in the diversion of $420 million in revenues, or only about 4 percent of 1973 postal revenues. It was never claimed that such a diversion would endanger universal service. See Board of Governors of the U.S. Postal Service, *Statutes Restricting the Private Carriage of Mail and Their Administration* (1973), reprinted, comm. print. 93-5, House Committee on Post Office and Civil Service (1973).

30. Cohen, Ferguson, and Xenakis, "Rural Delivery and the Universal Service Obligation."

31. Ibid, p.171. Specifically they found that in 1989 the city delivery cost per piece was only 8 percent lower than rural delivery but city delivery cost per delivery point was actually 7 percent higher than rural delivery cost; they concluded that there was no cross-subsidy of rural delivery by city delivery. That work was updated in their 1999 chapter, Cohen, Ferguson, Waller, and Xenakis, "Analysis of the Potential for Cream-Skimming."

32. The situation also implies that service quality levels are lower in rural areas because rural customers must supply the "last mile" of delivery at their own expense.

33. Cohen, Ferguson, and Xenakis, "Rural Delivery and the Universal Service Obligation," p. 170.

34. Ibid., p. 171.

35. Cohen, Ferguson, Waller, and Xenakis, "Analysis of the Potential for Cream-Skimming," pp. 143–44, note that "the real alternative delivery system in the United States is the newspaper industry which delivers advertising preprints or inserts." Also see Sidak and Spulber, *Protecting Competition,* p. 50: "Even rural areas are served by multiple newspaper delivery routes, which demonstrates that an extremely low-cost service can be maintained simply for the delivery of one item on a daily basis to a substantial proportion of households."

36. Andre Shleifer, "State versus Private Ownership," *Journal of Economic Perspectives* 12 (1998): 136.

37. In their concluding remarks, Cohen, Ferguson, and Xenakis, "Rural Delivery and the Universal Service Obligation," p. 171, state:

> It is no accident that, within the United States, United Parcel Service provides ubiquitous service for parcels. Federal Express and other overnight carriers do the same for overnight delivery. Moreover, the major long distance telephone carriers also provide ubiquitous service. Quite possibly, all of these common carriers find that sparsely settled portions of the country are unprofitable to serve. That these organizations provide universal service suggests that rural areas would receive postal service even absent a universal service requirement.

38. Cohen, Ferguson, Waller, and Xenakis, "Analysis of Potential for Cream-Skimming," p. 147. Additionally, mail aggregation businesses are likely to arise under competition to exploit economies of scale and scope obtaining from less frequent but more concentrated delivery. Potential mailers include magazines, advertisers, credit cards, banks, and utilities.

39. James I. Campbell Jr., response to written questions of Rep. John M. McHugh, *General Oversight of the U.S. Postal Service,* House Committee on Government Reform and Oversight Subcommittee on Postal Service 104th Congress., 1st sess., 552, 554–55 (Washington, D.C.: Government Printing Office, 1997).

40. See *Toward Postal Excellence,* p. 128.

41. Sidak and Spulber, *Protecting Competition,* p. 41.

42. U.S. Postal Service, *Statutes Restricting Private Carriage of Mail and their Administration,* House Committee on the Post Office and Civil Service, 93rd Cong., 1st sess., committee print 1973, pp. 9–10, 93–96. For a discussion, see Priest, "History of the Postal Monopoly," pp. 69–71.

43. See, for example, Bruce M. Owen, and Robert D. Willig, "Economics and Postal Pricing," in *The Future of the Postal Service,* edited by Joel L. Fleishman (Rockville, Md.: Aspen Institute, 1983); John C. Panzer, "Is Postal Service a Natural Monopoly?" in *Competition and Innovation in Postal Services,* edited by Michael A. Crew and Paul R. Kleindorfer (Amsterdam: Kluwer Academic Publishers, 1991); and Michael A. Crew and Paul R. Kleindorfer, *The Economics of Postal Service* (Boston: Kluwer Academic Publishers, 1992), p. 18.

44. Sidak and Spulber, *Protecting Competition,* p. 40.

45. Dennis Carlton and Jeffrey Perloff, *Modern Industrial Organization* (New York: Harper Collins, 1994), p. 58.

46. Sidak and Spulber, *Protecting Competition,* p. 42; and Carlton and Perloff, *Modern Industrial Organization,* p. 151.

47. John C. Moorhouse, *Electric Power: Deregulation and the Public Interest* (San Francisco: Pacific Research Institute, 1986).

48. Priest, "History of the Postal Monopoly," p. 71.

49. See, for example, Thomas W. Hazlett, and Matthew L. Spitzer, *Public Policy toward Cable Television: The Economics of Rate Controls* (Washington, D.C.: AEI Press, 1997); and Gregg A. Jarrell, "The Demand for State Regulation of the Electric Utility Industry," *Journal of Law and Economics* 21 (1978): 269–96.

50. In the context of the postal monopoly, natural monopoly theory suggests why we ought to have a postal monopoly, not why we actually have one. Policymakers would have to act in an irrational manner and ignore the interests of producers (in this case, the Postal Service) to enforce rates based on natural monopoly theory.

51. Harold Demsetz, "Why Regulate Utilities?" *Journal of Law and Economics* 11 (1968): 55–65.

52. William J. Baumol and Robert D. Willig, "Fixed Costs, Sunk Costs, Entry Barriers, and Sustainability of Monopoly," *Quarterly Journal of Economics* 96 (3) (August 1981): 405–31.

53. Elizabeth E. Bailey and John C. Panzar, "The Contestability of Airline Markets during the Transition to Deregulation," *Law and Contemporary Problems* 44 (1981): 125–45.

54. William J. Baumol, John C. Panzar, and Robert D. Willig, *Contestable Markets and the Theory of Industry Structure* (New York: Harcourt Brace Jovanovich, 1988), p. xiii.

55. Several studies have tested contestability theory; they include Don Coursey, Mark Isaac, and Vernon Smith, "Natural Monopoly and Contested Markets: Some Experimental Results," *Journal of Law and Economics* 27 (1984): 111, who used an experimental approach and found that

> the most significant result . . . is that the behavioral predictions of the contestable market hypothesis are fundamentally correct. It is simply not true that monopoly pricing is a "natural" result of a market merely because firms in the market exhibit decreasing costs and demand is sufficient to support no more than a single firm.

56. See Priest, "History of the Postal Monopoly," pp. 71–72, and Sidak and Spulber, *Protecting Competition*, pp. 43–60, for further criticism of the Postal Service's claims of natural monopoly.

57. *Washington Post*, September 23, 1996, p. A17.

58. Priest, "History of the Postal Monopoly," p. 79.

59. Miller, "End the Postal Monopoly," p. 150.

60. Campbell, "Introduction to the History of the Postal Monopoly Law," p. 9.

61. Sidak and Spulber, *Protecting Competition*, pp. 21–31.

62. See Sam Peltzman, "Toward a More General Theory of Regulation," *Journal of Law and Economics* 19 (1976): 211–40.

63. For an example of the phenomenon in a different industry, see Edmund W. Kitch, Marc Isaacson, and Daniel Kasper, "The Regulation of Taxicabs in Chicago," *Journal of Law and Economics* 14 (1971): 285.

64. "Lawmakers Put Chicks Transport up in the Air," *Wall Street Journal*, November 7, 2001, p. A24.

65. See, for example, 39 U.S.C. § 3623(d) (1973). An exception is standard mail B (formerly fourth-class mail), which is priced according to zones.

66. See Robert H. Cohen, "Consequences of Competition," in *Mail @ the Millennium*, edited by Edward L. Hudgins (Washington, D.C.: Cato Institute, 2000); Cohen, Ferguson, and Xenakis, "Rural Delivery and the Universal

Service Obligation"; and Cohen, Ferguson, Waller, and Xenakis, "Analysis of Potential for Cream-Skimming."

67. Priest, "History of the Postal Monopoly," p. 70.

68. Ibid., p. 72.

69. See President's Commission on Postal Reorganization, *Toward Postal Excellence*, p. 129. The statements were made before inexpensive computers, software, and point-of-sale devices were widely available and have less traction today. I discuss the impact of technological change on the USPS in detail in chapter 5.

70. See, for example, Ronald H. Coase, "The Economics of Uniform Pricing Systems," *Manchester School of Economics and Social Studies* 15 (1947): 139–56.

71. Sam Peltzman, "The Economic Theory of Regulation after a Decade of Deregulation," *Brookings Papers: Microeconomics* 1989:

> Suppose a regulated firm, *X*, sells to two customers, *A* and *B*. Suppose further that *A* and *B* have equal demands and equal political weight (that is, their utility enters the regulator's utility function in the same way), but that the marginal cost *(MC)* is higher for serving *A* than for serving *B*. Now recall the general result that *X* will not get maximum profits; for simplicity call this "tax" on maximum profits, *T*, and assume it is fixed. Since *X* cares only about the size of *T*, not its distribution among *A* and *B*, and since *A* and *B* are politically equal, the regulator has only one remaining task: to make the price *(P)* to *A* and *B* *(P_A* and *P_B)*, and thereby *A*'s and *B*'s consumer surplus, as nearly equal as possible, given *T*. The result will be a lower P_A/MC_A than P_B/MC_B. If *T* is big enough to permit it, the regulator will completely ignore the fact that $MC_A \neq MC_B$ and set $P_A = P_B$. While there are inevitable complications and ambiguities, this tendency for the high cost customer to get the low *P/MC* is common.

72. The Postal Service is often referred to as a government-owned enterprise, and I use that appellation here. There are, however, no actual ownership shares. It remains an establishment of the executive branch and is thus only a government-owned enterprise in the same limited sense as the Department of Defense, for example. See Pub. L. 91-375, August 12, 1970, 84 Stat. 720.

73. President's Commission on Postal Reorganization, *Toward Postal Excellence*, pp. 53–54.

74. Importantly, the commission questioned only the *feasibility of transferring* ownership, not the ultimate desirability of private ownership of postal services.

75. "Shares Rose 2.4% on Debut Day for Deutsche Post," *New York Times*, November 21, 2000, p. C10. The Dutch post office has similarly privatized. Additionally there have been successful privatizations of large telecommunications

firms, including British Telecom, Deutsche Telekom, Telefonica, Telstra, and Telmex. Given the major privatizations in the United Kingdom and elsewhere over the past twenty years, it is doubtful that a similar arguments would be made today.

76. Tierney, *U.S. Postal Service*, p. 32.

77. Because the Postal Service does not have to pay out earnings according to this statutory requirement, "free cash flows," or cash flows in excess of those needed to fund all positive net present value projects, are created. Free cash flows create particularly severe agency problems. See Michael C. Jensen, "Takeovers: Their Causes and Consequences," *Journal of Economic Perspectives* 2 (1988): 21–48

78. The Post Office ran deficits every year from 1945 to 1970; they were considered an expense of the Post Office Department, financed directly from the Treasury. See Ewing and Salaman, *The Postal Crisis,* pp. 6–7.

79. 39 U.S.C. § 3621.

80. USPS, *Annual Report of the United States Postal Service,* various years.

81. Public Law 94-421, 90 Stat. 1303 (1976) (codified at 39 U.S.C. 2401 (d)) (1976). See S. 966, 94th Cong., 2d sess. (1976) *U.S. Code Cong. and Admin. News,* 1976, p. 2400.

82. USPS, *1997 Annual Report of the Postmaster General.*

83. 39 U.S.C. § 2005. Those statutes limit both the total amount and the annual borrowing capacity of the USPS.

84. 39 U.S.C. §§ 2006 (a), (c).

85. Paul W. MacAvoy and George S. McIsaac, "The Current File on the Case for Privatization of the Federal Government Enterprises," in *Deregulation and Privatization in the United States,* Hume Papers on Public Policy, vol. 3, no. 3., edited by Paul W. MacAvoy (Edinburgh: Edinburgh University Press, 1995), state:

> The public enterprises have had special access to capital through the Federal Financial Bank (FFB) which guarantees public bonds at interest charges less than market rates for private companies of comparable risk. Both TVA and USPS financed their placements of debt with the FFB at a 12.5 basis-point premium above Treasury bond rates. This rate was lower than on bonds of companies with comparable financial performance. . . . If these organizations had not had access to FFB financing, the additional interest charges which they would have incurred would have exceeded $5 billion over the first half of the 1980s.

86. Sidak and Spulber, *Protecting Competition,* p. 97, n. 34.

87. Ibid., pp. 86–87. See also USPS, *1998 Annual Report,* p. 32.

88. 39 U.S.C. § 401 (9).

89. 39 U.S.C. §§ 3601, 3624 (1970).

90. Ibid.

91. 39 U.S.C. § 3622.

92. 39 U.S.C. § 3621, 3622, 3626 (1970).

93. See *Quarterly Financial Report Program*, Public Law 101-227, § 3(a), 103 Stat. 1943, 1944 (1989), codified at 39 U.S.C. § 2005(a).

94. 39 U.S.C. § 3661 (b).

95. 39 U.S.C. § 3625 (a),(d).

96. *New York Times*, October 1, 1981, p. A1.

97. "Postal Service to Raise Rates on Most Classes," *Wall Street Journal*, May 9, 2001, p. A2. Although the board has used the power only twice in twenty-five years, its existence may be more important than its use, as such power may have a "chilling effect" on the commission's decisions.

98. Paul L. Joskow, "Regulatory Failure, Regulatory Reform, and Structural Change in the Electric Power Industry," *Brookings Papers on Economic Activity, Microeconomics* (1989), for example, shows that the equity of investor-owned electric utilities in the late 1970s was reduced by failure to increase rates adequately.

99. In his 1994 testimony the Postal Service's main revenue witness, John H. Ward (Tr. 5/2236) stated, "Despite maximum allowable annual borrowing for operating and capital purposes ($1 billion for operating purposes and $2 billion for capital purposes - net), the end-of-year cash and investment balances would be less than the amount necessary to fund one bi-weekly payroll (currently about $1.1 billion)."

100. On July 25, 1990, the Postal Rate Commission formally advised the USPS of its opinion that it should not implement a plan to downgrade nationwide first-class delivery standards. (*Summary of Postal Rate Commission Advisory Opinion on First-Class Delivery Standards Realignment*, N89-1, July 25, 1990). On July 26, 1990, Postmaster General Anthony Frank responded in a letter that "after consideration of the opinion, we have concluded that it does not warrant changing our scheduled Saturday implementation of overnight standard changes" (letter of the postmaster general to the chairman of the Postal Rate Commission, July 26, 1990, copy on file with the author). See also Sidak and Spulber, *Protecting Competition*, p. 50.

101. A public utility commission, in contrast, has control over such variables as the reliability of electric power by linking allowed rates of return to outages. Additionally, performance standards for a privately owned regulated utility are expressly stated. In telecommunications, for example, such details as time until dial tone, length of repair waits, and speed of infrastructure expansion are expressly specified. See J. Gregory Sidak and Daniel F. Spulber, *Deregulatory Takings and the Regulatory Contract* (Cambridge: Cambridge University Press, 1997).

102. Clyde S. DuPont, "The Postal Rate Commission," in *Perspectives on Postal Service Issues*, edited by Roger Sherman (Washington, D.C.: American Enterprise Institute, 1980), p. 115.

103. Tierney, *U.S. Postal Service*, p. 210.

104. In *National Association of Greeting Card Publishers* (1976, pp. 587–88), the Court, referring to cross-subsidies from first-class mail, states, "In seeking postal reform through the 1970 Act it was a central and express aim of both Houses of Congress to end the abuses of this practice." See William T. Mayton, "The Missions and Methods of the Postal Power," in *Governing the Postal Service*, edited by J. Gregory Sidak (Washington, D.C.: AEI Press, 1994), p. 102.

105. Ewing and Salaman, *The Postal Crisis*, p. 31, report that "it is widely accepted that first class mail subsidizes other classes. Postal Service statistics support this viewpoint." Additionally Sidak and Spulber, *Protecting Competition*, p. 120, state, "The Post Office's ratemaking procedures repeatedly produced cross-subsidies running from first class mail to other mail services."

106. 39 U.S.C. § 3622(b)(3).

107. See, for example, William J. Baumol and David F. Bradford, "Optimal Departures from Marginal Cost Pricing," *American Economic Review* 60 (1970): 265–83.

108. In his original article Ramsey clearly assumes pure competition. See Frank P. Ramsey, "A Contribution to the Theory of Taxation," *Economic Journal* 37 (1927): 47–61.

109. See Sidak and Spulber, *Protecting Competition*, pp. 126–33.

110. *National Association of Greeting Card Publishers* (1976), pp. 585-86; and *National Association of Greeting Card Publishers v. United States Postal Service*, 607 F.2d 392 (D.C. Cir 1978). See also Mayton, "Missions and Methods," pp. 102–4.

111. *National Association of Greeting Card Publishers v. United States Postal Service*, 462 U.S. 810 (1983). Researchers have noted the difficulty of allocating common costs in any event. For example, Miller, "End the Postal Monopoly," p. 151, states, "The existence of large common costs in enterprises like the Postal Service makes it impossible to allocate total costs to individual services in a nonarbitrary manner."

112. Tierney, *Postal Reorganization*, p. 124, states:

> The net effect of the postal costing and pricing methods has been to permit the Postal Service to place an inappropriate share of the rate burden on first-class mail, which to date has a less elastic demand than other classes largely because the Postal Service has a legal monopoly over it. . . . Because the Postal Service's short-run costing method classifies buildings and equipment as "fixed" costs, the Postal Service is able to charge 58 per cent of the costs of this bulk-

mail system to first-class mail, even though none of these facilities
is used to handle first-class mail.

113. "Chief Administrative Law Judge's Initial Decision," in *Postal Rate and
Fee Increases,* docket R74-1, vol. 1, pp. 1–4.

114. 39 U.S.C. § 202, (1970). The appointment procedure was an attempt
to emulate that of CEOs of private corporations. See Mayton, "Missions and
Methods," p. 90.

115. See R. Richard Geddes, "Agency Costs and Governance in the United
States Postal Service in Governing the Postal Service," edited by J. Gregory
Sidak (Washington, D.C.: AEI Press, 1994), for a more complete elucidation of
this concept. The concept is not alien to U.S. institutional arrangements. The
citizens of Alaska, for example, receive a substantial annual dividend check for
their share of the royalties that the state receives from North Slope oil drilling;
the situation implies a partial ownership interest. See "Drill, Say Alaskans, Who
Know Their Pockets Are Lined with Oil," *New York Times,* March 18, 2001, p. 14.

116. See Eugene F. Fama and Michael C. Jensen, "Separation of Ownership
and Control," *Journal of Law and Economics* 26 (1983): 301–26.

117. The topic is discussed in detail in Neal Devins, "Tempest in an
Envelope," *UCLA Law Review* 41 (1994): 1035–62.

118. See *Humphrey's Executor v. United States,* 295 U.S. 602 (1935), and the
literature associated with that case. See also Sidak and Spulber, *Protecting
Competition,* p. 96.

119. "Bush Reportedly Threatens Postal Board over Rate Rise," *New York
Times,* January 5, 1993, p. A11. The president's power to remove officials may
be more important than the power of appointment. See also Sidak and Spulber,
Protecting Competition, p. 96.

120. "Bush Temporarily Prevented from Dismissing Postmaster," *New York
Times,* January 8, 1993, p. A13; *Mackie v. Bush,* 809 F. Supp. 144 (D.D.C. 1993).

121. "Bush Defies Judge and Names New Member to Postal Board," *New
York Times,* January 9, 1993, p. I10.

122. "Court Blocks Dismissal of Postal Governors," *New York Times,* January
17, 1993, p. I22.

123. The first raise was enacted as the Federal Employees Salary Act of
1970, Public Law 91-231, § 2(a)(1), 84 Stat. 195 (1970), while the second was
included in the Postal Reorganization and Pay Adjustment Act, Pub. L. No. 91-
375, § 9, 84 Stat. 719, 784 (1970).

124. 39 U.S.C. §§ 9, 1201-09.

125. Fleishman, *Future of the Postal Service,* p. 99. The number of unionized
workers has increased since then. Nonunionized workers represented by
professional associations include the National League of Postmasters (representing rural postmasters), the National Association of Postmasters (representing urban postmasters), and the National Association of Postal Supervisors

(representing approximately 35,000 middle-management supervisors). J. Walsh and G. Mangum, *Labor Struggle in the Post Office: From Selective Lobbying to Collective Bargaining* (Armonk, N.Y.: M. E. Sharpe, 1992), p. 35. See also Mayton, "Missions and Methods," p. 107.

126. D. G. Fowler, *Unmailable: Congress and the Post Office* (Athens: University of Georgia Press, 1977). Employees with less than six years on the job can be laid off.

127. 39 U.S.C. § 1003(a).

128. Sharon P. Smith, "Are Postal Workers Over- or Underpaid?" *Industrial Relations* 15 (1976): 168–76; and Sharon P. Smith, *Equal Pay in the Public Sector: Fact or Fancy?* (Princeton:, Princeton University Press, 1977).

129. Douglas K. Adie, "How Have the Postal Workers Fared Since the 1970 Act?" in *Perspectives on Postal Service Issues,* p. 75, edited by Roger Sherman (Washington, D.C.: American Enterprise Institute, 1980).

130. Jeffrey M. Perloff and Michael L. Watcher, "Wage Comparability in the U.S. Postal Service," *Industrial and Labor Relations Review* 38 (1984): 26–35.

131. Michael L. Wachter and Jeffrey M. Perloff, "A Comparative Analysis of Wage Premiums and Industrial Relations in the British Post Office and the United States Postal Service," in *Competition and Innovation in Postal Services,* edited by Michael A. Crew and Paul R. Kleindorfer (Amsterdam: Kluwer Academic Publishers, 1991).

132. B. T. Hirsch, M. L. Wachter, and J. W. Gillula, "Postal Service Compensation and the Comparability Standard," *Research in Labor Economics* 18 (1999): 243–79. When occupational skill requirements and working conditions are accounted for, the premium increases to 34 percent.

133. 39 U.S.C. § 2401(b).

134. Sidak and Spulber, *Protecting Competition,* p. 95; Tierney, *U.S. Postal Service,* p. 225. Short of additional reorganization, however, it appears that Congress has little power to actually intervene in postal operations.

135. Tierney, *U.S. Postal Service,* p. 223.

136. Ibid.

137. 39 U.S.C. § 2008(a).

138. Sharon M. Oster, "The Failure of Postal Reform," in *Deregulation and Privatization in the United States,* vol. 3, Hume Papers on Public Policy, edited by Paul W. MacAvoy (Edinburgh: Edinburgh University Press, 1995), pp. 114–15.

139. Sidak and Spulber, *Protecting Competition,* p.100.

140. Ralph Nader, "Price Fixing by the Postal Service," *Nation,* December 12, 1981, p. 631. See also Richard Meyer, "Care for a Spin in My Chateau, Postmaster?" *Washington Monthly,* February 16, 1984, p. 54.

Chapter 4: Postal Reorganization Act

1. Sam Peltzman, "The Control and Performance of State-Owned Enterprises: Comment," in *Privatization and State-Owned Enterprises,* edited by Paul W. MacAvoy, W. Stanbury, G. Yarrow, and R. Zeckhauser (Boston: Kluwer Academic Publishers, 1989) pp. 69–75.

2. Paul W. MacAvoy, and George S. McIsaac, "The Performance and Management of United States Federal Government Corporations," in *Privatization and State-Owned Enterprises,* edited by Paul W. MacAvoy, W. Stanbury, G. Yarrow, and R. Zeckhauser (Boston: Kluwer Academic Publishers 1989), p. 89.

3. Donald R. Ewing and Roger K. Salaman, *The Postal Crisis: The Postal Function as a Communications Service,* Office of Telecommunications Special Publication 77-13, (Washington, D.C.: Department of Commerce, Office of Telecommunications, 1977).

4. The USPS recently instituted a new mail classification system. USPS, *1996 Annual Report,* pp. 39–41. Because the majority of the sample years are under the old system, I refer to the old system throughout.

5. The two differ because of "casual" and seasonal employees. That difference allows examination of productivity differences between career and total employees.

6. A series is covariance stationary if the mean and all auto-covariances are not affected by a change in time origin. Walter Enders, *Applied Econometric Time-Series* (New York: John Wiley, 1995), pp. 68–71. Nonstationarity can produce a "spurious regressions" problem. See C. Granger and P. Newbold, "Spurious Regressions in Econometrics," *Journal of Econometrics* 2 (1974): 111–20.

7. Enders, *Applied Econometric Time-Series,* pp. 212–21.

8. The maximum number of lags was arbitrarily chosen as ten.

9. Critical values for these t-statistics were compared with those reported in Pierre Perron, "The Great Crash, the Oil Shock, and the Unit Root Hypothesis," *Econometrica* 57 (1989), 1376–401, t. 4. B. Critical values depend on the proportion of observations that come before the break, or λ, for each variable. For most series examined here, that value is 3.76 at the 5 percent confidence level. Such tests typically have low power to distinguish between a unit root and a near-unit root process and too often indicate a unit root. See Enders, *Applied Econometric Time-Series,* pp. 251–52.

10. Because unit root tests have lower power to distinguish between unit root and near-unit root processes, rejection of a unit root is strong evidence of a stationary series. See Enders, *Applied Econometric Time-Series,* p. 251.

11. Because the intercept reveals a deterministic time-trend in the differenced series, a separate time-trend is unnecessary.

12. Enders, *Applied Econometric Time-Series,* pp. 270–75.

13. See Perron, "Great Crash, Oil Shock, and Unit Root Hypothesis," p. 1363.

14. An alternative approach is to allow the data to determine the correct number of breaks. See Tony Caporale and Kevin Grier, "Political Regime Change and the Real Interest Rate," *Journal of Money, Credit and Banking* 32 (3) (pt. 1) (August 2000): 320–34.

15. Other potential tests for unit roots require splitting the sample into two subperiods and using Dickey-Fuller tests. Those actions greatly reduce the degrees of freedom. Enders, *Applied Econometric Time-Series*, pp. 245. Accounting for nonstationarity in a separate regression may also result in inadequate control for structural change, which can lead to the use of excessive lags. See Robin L. Lumsdaine and Serena Ng, "Testing for ARCH in the Presence of a Possibly Misspecified Conditional Mean," *Journal of Econometrics* 93 (1999): 257–79.

16. The inclusion of more recent price data may reveal a return to increasing real first-class prices.

17. George S. Tolley, "Direct Testimony of George S. Tolley on Behalf of United States Postal Service, Postal Rate and Fee Changes," 1994 (Docket R94-1), at 185.

18. David E. M. Sappington and J. Gregory Sidak, *Incentives Anticompetitive for Behavior by Public Enterprises*, AEI-Brookings Joint Center for Regulatory Studies, Working Paper 99-11, Washington, D.C. (1999), show that a government-owned enterprise will have the incentive to engage in that behavior if it maximizes a combination of revenues and profits.

19. That is only one explanation among many for the apparent downturn in relative postal salaries since the mid-1980s. Public sector unions generally lost power during the period.

20. There is little evidence, however, that the act resulted in more postal workers. Time-series tests suggest that the act had no effect on either WORKER1 or WORKER2.

21. See Ewing and Salaman, *Postal Crisis*, p. 25. That is also consistent with rising union membership in the Postal Service, rather than declining as in many other sectors. See George L. Priest, "Socialism, Eastern Europe, and the Question of the Postal Monopoly," in *Governing the Postal Service*, edited by J. Gregory Sidak (Washington, D.C.: AEI Press, 1994), p. 51.

22. In the case of one output and many inputs, the ratio of output to weighted average input requirement shows the production productivity or "total factor productivity" (TFP). The Postal Service itself used pieces of mail per workyear as its measure of productivity until 1985, when it switched to total factor productivity. See D. C. Christensen, L. R. Christensen, C. E. Guy, and D. J. O'Hara, "U.S. Postal Service Productivity: Measurement and Performance," in *Regulation and the Nature of Postal and Delivery Services*, edited by Michael A.

Crew and Paul R. Kleindorfer (Amsterdam: Kluwer Academic Publishers, 1993).

23. Postal appropriations have begun to rise again in recent years.

24. The "taxpayers' equity" variable refers to the value of the Postal Service's assets minus its liabilities. Because of difficulties in the Postal Service's accounting on both the assets and the liabilities side of the balance sheet, as discussed in chapter 6, the variable should be interpreted with caution.

Chapter 5: A Case for Postal Reform

1. Robert W. Hahn and John A. Hird, "The Costs and Benefits of Regulation: Review and Synthesis," *Yale Journal of Regulation* 8 (1991): 233–78.

2. Thomas M. Lenard, "The Efficiency Effects of the Postal Monopoly: The Case of Third-Class Mail," *Journal of Regulatory Economics* 6 (1994): 421–32.

3. Adolph Berle and Gardiner Means, *The Modern Corporation and Private Property* (New York: Macmillan, 1937).

4. Eugene Fama and Michael Jensen, "Organizational Forms and Investment Decisions," *Journal of Financial Economics* 14 (1985): 101–19.

5. Eugene F. Fama and Michael C. Jensen, "Separation of Ownership and Control," *Journal of Law and Economics* 26 (1983): 301–25.

6. Eirik Furubotn and Rudolf Richter, "The New Institutional Economics: An Assessment," in *The New Institutional Economics,* edited by Eirik Furubotn and Rudolf Richter (College Station: Texas A&M Press, 1991), p. 1.

7. The de facto residual claimants of the government firm become the politically influential groups discussed in chapter 4.

8. See, for example, Anne T. Coughlan and Ronald M. Schmidt, "Executive Compensation, Management Turnover, and Firm Performance," *Journal of Accounting and Economics* 7 (1985): 43–66; Michael Weisbach, "Outside Directors and CEO Turnover," *Journal of Financial Economics* 20 (1988): 431–92; Jerold B. Warner, Robb L. Watts, and Karen H. Wruck, "Stock Prices and Top Management Changes," *Journal of Financial Economics* 20 (1988): 461.

9. See generally Eugene Fama, "Contract Costs and Financing Decisions," *Journal of Business* 63 (supp. 1990): S71–91.

10. Ibid., p. S87.

11. See Harold Demsetz and Kenneth Lehn, "The Structure of Corporate Ownership: Causes and Consequences," *Journal of Political Economy* 93 (1985): 1155–77.

12. That scenario assumes that ownership is concentrated in the hands of a single manager.

13. See Henry Manne, "Mergers and the Market for Corporate Control," *Journal of Political Economy* 73 (1965): 110–20.

14. Michael Jensen and Richard Ruback, "The Market for Corporate Control: The Scientific Evidence," *Journal of Financial Economics* 11 (1983): 5–50; Gregg

Jarrell, James Brickley, and Jeffrey Netter, "The Market for Corporate Control: The Evidence since 1980," *Journal of Economic Perspectives* 2 (1988): 49–68.

15. Takeovers of government firms are invariably of a high-cost form through elections or revolutions.

16. See, for example, Kevin J. Murphy, "Corporate Performance and Managerial Remuneration: An Empirical Analysis," *Journal of Accounting and Economics* 7 (1985): 11–41; Coughlan and Schmidt, "Executive Compensation."

17. Warner, Watts, and Wruck, "Stock Prices and Top Management Changes," find that managerial removals are correlated with a firm's stock returns, but only if performance is extremely good or bad. Like signals from the product market, managerial turnover may occur too late to warn shareholders of risks associated with their ownership stake.

18. Because the Postal Service's current equity position is negative, taxpayers actually owe money as a result of their ownership in the government enterprise.

19. In practice, government firms may be subject to the government service (GS) pay scale, which limits linkages between pay and performance.

20. Although accounting information may provide a measure of implied owner wealth in government firms, without the right to the residual it is doubtful that owners would ever benefit from increases in those measures.

21. See, for example, Franklin M. Fisher and John J. McGowan, "On the Misuse of Accounting Rates of Return to Infer Monopoly Profits," *American Economic Review* 73 (1983): 82–94.

22. The incentive to maximize the value of the residual claim also provides the incentive to minimize costs. Conversely the lack of clear property rights results in inefficiency. For example, Tierney, *Postal Reorganization*, p. vii, states: "As the following pages document, much of what citizens regard as inefficiency or ineffectiveness in the operation of public agencies stems not from managerial incompetence but from the obligation of most government agencies to pursue multiple goals and to serve multiple interests, all of which may be conflicting or even irreconcilable."

23. Jeffrey N. Gordon, "The Contestable Claims of Shareholder Wealth Maximization: Evidence from the Airline Industry," paper prepared for the Columbia Law School/NYU law and economics workshop (2000), p. 1.

24. Tierney, *U.S. Postal Service*, p. 2.

25. Clifford Winston, "Economic Deregulation: Days of Reckoning for Microeconomists," *Journal of Economic Literature* 31 (1993): 1263–89, t 1, provides a summary of the major reform initiatives in each of these industries.

26. John C. Panzer, "Competition, Efficiency, and the Vertical Structure of Postal Services," in *Regulation and the Nature of Postal Services,* edited by Michael A. Crew and Paul R. Kleindorfer (Amsterdam: Kluwer Academic Publishers, 1993), p. 91.

27. Winston, "Economic Deregulation," p. 1263.

28. Robert W. Crandall and Jerry Ellig, *Economic Deregulation and Customer Choice: Lessons for the Electric Utility Industry* (Fairfax: Center for Market Processes, 1997), p. 9.

29. The industries were chosen because they are similar to postal services in structure. Winston examined industries such as banking and brokerage that were unlikely to share postal service's network characteristics to the same degree.

30. Winston, "Economic Deregulation."

31. Crandall and Ellig, *Economic Deregulation and Customer Choice.*

32. Ibid., p. 34.

33. Residential prices fell by 32 percent, commercial by 38 percent, electric utility by 60 percent, and "city gate" by 52 percent. The differences are explained by costs of transportation and "interruptibility." Ibid., pp. 10–11.

34. There is, however, some evidence that consumer welfare gains in telecommunications originate from quasi-rents extracted from incumbent producers through regulatory opportunism. See Jerry A. Hausman and J. Gregory Sidak, "A Consumer-Welfare Approach to the Mandatory Unbundling of Telecommunications Networks," *Yale Law Journal* 109 (1999): 417–505.

35. Postal service is more labor-intensive than many other network industries; that factor may help explain these differences. Labor intensity, however, is itself a function of government ownership, as mentioned above.

36. See Winston, *Economic Deregulation,* p. 1269, t. 2, for a description of the major distortions introduced by regulation. The number of industries in which prices were set above marginal cost is striking.

37. Clifford Winston, "U.S. Industry Adjustment to Economic Deregulation," *Journal of Economic Perspectives* 12 (1998): 91.

38. Nancy Rose, "The Incidence of Regulatory Rents in the Motor Carrier Industry," *Rand Journal of Economics* 16 (1985): 299–318, examined the distribution of the losses from trucking deregulation.

39. That hiring is more likely to be applicable to mail carriers than to mail clerks, for example.

40. Winston examined additional industries besides those discussed here. Estimates of total social gains are higher if firms are assumed to adjust optimally to deregulation. See Winston, "Economic Deregulation," p. 1284.

41. Winston, "U.S. Industry Adjustment," pp. 95–96. Empirical evidence indicates that deregulation of airlines improved corporate governance through more concentrated ownership, increased stock option grants to managers, and smaller board sizes. See Stacey R. Kole and Kenneth M. Lehn, "Deregulation and the Adaptation of Governance Structure: The Case of the U.S. Airline Industry," *Journal of Financial Economics* 52 (1999): 79–117.

42. Winston, "U.S. Industry Adjustment," p. 98.

43. Ibid., p. 89.

44. Ibid., p. 108

45. James I. Campbell Jr., "The Postal Monopoly Law: A Historical Perspective," in *The Last Monopoly: Privatizing the Postal Service for the Information Age,* edited by Edward L. Hudgins (Washington, D.C.: Cato Institute, 1996), p. 11.

46. Ibid., p. 13.

47. USPS, *1998 Annual Report.*

48. USPS, *1998 Annual Report.* Also see Michael A. Crew and Paul R. Kleindorfer, *The Economics of Postal Service* (Amsterdam: Kluwer Academic Publishers, 1992), pp. 8–10.

49. "Postal Service Soon to Let Two Firms Nationally Sell Computer-Made Stamps," *Wall Street Journal,* July 19, 1999, p. B10.

50. For example, the USPS, *1998 Annual Report* (Management Discussion and Analysis section) states:

> The increasingly sophisticated use of data allows businesses to go beyond using the mail as a targeted advertising medium to a personalized means of building lasting business relationships. Declining computing costs along with rapid innovation in data base management and demographic analysis contributed to a rapid growth in mail volume in the 1980s. These developments, combined with the introduction of work-sharing discounts, which helped mailers take advantage of these trends, caused an explosion in mail volume.

51. Sidak and Spulber, *Protecting Competition,* pp. 20–21.

52. George S. Tolley, "Direct Testimony of George S. Tolley on Behalf of United States Postal Service," *Postal Rate and Fee Changes,* 1994 (docket R94-1), pp 28–30.

53. USPS, *1996 Annual Report,* pp. 39–40.

54. Frank A. Wolak, "Electronic Substitution in the Household-Level Demand for Postal Delivery Services," in *A Communications Cornucopia: Markle Foundation Essays on Information Policy,* edited by Rogert G. Noll and Monroe E. Price (Washington, D.C.: Brookings Institution Press, 1998).

55. For details of the technology, see Jerry A. Hausman, J. Gregory Sidak, and Hal J. Singer, "Cable Modems and DSL: Broadband Internet Access for Residential Customers," *American Economic Association Papers and Proceedings* 91 (2001): 302–7; and Jerry A. Hausman, J. Gregory Sidak, and Hal J. Singer, "Residential Demand for Broadband Telecommunications and Consumer Access to Unaffiliated Internet Content Providers," *Yale Journal on Regulation* 18 (2001): 129–73.

56. USPS, *1996 Annual Report,* p. 40.

57. Ibid.

58. William J. Henderson, statement of postmaster general and chief executive officer, United States Postal Service, before the Subcommittee on the Postal

Service, Committee on Government Reform, U.S. House of Representatives, September 19, 2000.

59. See W. Kip Viscusi, John Vernon, and Joseph E. Harrington, *Economics of Regulation and Antitrust*, 2nd ed. (Cambridge: MIT Press, 1995), pp. 351–53, for an example from the telecommunications industry.

60. Ibid. p. 353.

Chapter 6: Global Postal Reform

1. For a more complete overview, see Organization for Economic Cooper-ation and Development Directorate for Financial, Fiscal, and Monetary Affairs, Committee on Competition Law and Policy, *Promoting Competition in Postal Ser-vices*, DAFFE/CLP 22 (1999): 99. Also see James I. Campbell Jr., "The Global Postal Reform Movement," in *Mail @ the Millennium* (Washington, D.C.: Cato Institute, 2000), and James I. Campbell Jr., "Modern Postal Reform Laws: A Comparative Survey," in *Postal and Delivery Services: Pricing, Productivity, Regulation, and Strategy*, edited by Michael A. Crew and Paul R. Kleindorfer (Boston: Kluwer Academic Publishers, 2002). The discussion borrows heavily from those sources.

2. See Campbell, "Global Postal Reform Movement," for an overview.

3. If the *postal monopoly* is defined as a certain fixed monetary amount (say a multiple of the stamp price), then inflation alone will erode the scope of the monopoly, assuming that stamp prices do not also rise with inflation.

4. See http://www.nzpost.net.nz/nzpost/control/corporate/contract/disclosure.

5. See http://www.nzpost.net.nz/nzpost/control/corporate/deregulationt/facts.

6. See USPS, *2000 Annual Performance Plan*, at E5.

7. U.S. Postal Service, *Transformation Plan* (Washington, D.C.: Government Printing Office, 2002), H-23.

8. Ibid.

9. See http://www.auspost.com.au/mediacentre/index.asp? link_id=4.22.

10. National Competition Council, *Review of the Australian Postal Corporation Act*, vol. 2 (Washington, D.C.: NCC, 1998), p. 392.

11. *Finland Post Annual Report 2000* (Helskini: Finland Post, 2000), avail-able at http://www.posti.fi/findlandpost/annualreports/ann2000/indexe2000.html.

12. Ibid.

13. See http://www.npt.no/eng/publications/annual_reports/arsrapport99/postal.html, accessed 2/9/2002.

14. "Shares Rose 2.4% on Debut Day for Deutsche Post," *New York Times*, November 21, 2000, p. C10.

15. "Path Clear for Sale of Deutsche Post," *Financial Times*, U.S. ed., July 26, 2001, p. 2.

16. See Matthias Finger and Colette Friedli, "The Swiss Postal Law of 1998: Is It Worth the Monopoly Protection?" in *Emerging Competition in Postal*

and Delivery Services, edited by Michael A. Crew and Paul R. Kleindorfer (Boston: Kluwer Academic Publishers, 1999), p. 32.

17. Ibid., p. 36.

18. Ibid., p. 41.

19. Finger and Friedli, "Swiss Postal Law," p. 40, states:

> Also, articles 14 and 15 of the Postal Law say that *prices for reserved services* have to be approved by the Department, and such prices do not necessarily have to be based on actual costs, nor do they have to reflect the market price. In addition and more generally, the prices of the universal services have restrictions attached to them, as they must be the same in all parts of the country and moreover "reasonable." This is somewhat contradictory and as elsewhere it is said that prices have to be economic in nature.

20. See James I. Campbell Jr., "Postal Monopoly Law."

21. For a detailed discussion of reforms in the United Kingdom, from which the brief survey borrows, see Campbell, "Modern Postal Reform Laws."

22. U.K. Post Act, §§ 3–5, 125.

23. USPS, *Transformation Plan,* H-9.

24. Goeff Gibbs, "Consignia Consigned to the Bin," *Guardian,* June 14, 2002.

25. Terry Macalister, "Consignia Faces Threat from Dutch," *Guardian,* August 6, 2002.

26. Costs of introducing competition include anticompetitive behavior by the government-owned (or previously government-owned) incumbent. Examples include behavior by Deutsche Post and by Sweden Post.

27. The European Union, for example, decided after years of study that it would define *universal service* as ensuring delivery for all citizens at *affordable* postage rates. It would therefore not guarantee a uniform rate throughout Europe. See Campbell response, pp. 522, 554–55.

Chapter 7: A Proposal for Postal Reform

1. Douglas K. Adie, *Monopoly Mail: Privatizing the U.S. Postal Service* (New York: Transaction Publishers, 1989), pp. 153–54.

2. See Alan Robinson and David Rawnsley, "USPS Finances: Is There a Financially Viable Future?" in *Postal and Delivery Services: Pricing, Productivity, Regulation and Strategy,* edited by Michael A. Crew and Paul R. Kleindorfer (Amsterdam: Kluwer Academic Publishers, 2001).

3. Ibid.

4. Ibid.

5. William J. Henderson, "End of the Route: I Ran the Postal Service; It Should be Privatized," *Washington Post,* September 2, 2001, p. B1. A detailed estimate of the Postal Service's net value is an enormous undertaking, outside the scope of this book.

6. The recent discovery by the Office of Personnel Management of billions of dollars of USPS overpayments into its pension fund highlights the point. See Stephen Barr, "Despite Windfall of Billions, Postal Service to Keep Cutting Costs." *Washington Post,* November 8, 2002, p. B2.

7. As Postmaster General Henderson has suggested, however, employees now realize that the USPS is threatened by technological change, and therefore may be less resistant to change. Ibid.

8. Employee grievances are costly for the USPS. About 126,000 employee grievances and arbitration cases are pending, or one for every six postal workers represented by the union. "Postal Service Seeks to Hand Over Some Bias Disputes to Third Party," *Wall Street Journal,* July 27, 2001, p. A2.

9. Henderson, "End of the Route."

10. Other researchers have advocated this basic reform. For example, John T. Tierney, in *U.S. Postal Service,* p. 210, writes:

> The single most important defect in the institutional arrangement for postal rate-making is that the Postal Rate Commission does not have final authority over rates . . . It hardly seems an acceptable situation that a government agency enjoying a monopoly over certain of its services has the ultimate power to put into effect whatever rates it chooses, irrespective of the recommendations of the independent Postal Rate Commission . . . A far better, and certainly more streamlined, arrangement would be to give final authority to the Postal Rate Commission.

The Postal Service's recent overruling of the commission suggests that such a change would indeed have a constraining effect on postal rates.

11. For examples of the problem with respect to Deutsche Post, see *Commission Initiates Proceedings against Deutsche Post AG for Abuse of a Dominant Position,* IP/00/919 (Brussels: European Commission, August 8, 2000); and *Antitrust Proceedings in the Postal Sector Result in Deutsche Post Separating Competitive Parcel Services from Letter Monopoly,* IP 01/419 (Brussels: European Commission, March 29, 2001).

12. A congressional postal reform bill, H.R. 22, suggested that type of regulation. See Robert Taub, "Congressional Plans for Postal Modernization," in *Mail @ the Millennium,* edited by Edward L. Hudgins (Washington, D.C.: Cato Institute, 2000).

13. See Michael A. Crew and Paul R. Kleindorfer, "Privatizing the U.S. Postal Service," in *Mail @ the Millennium*, edited by Edward L. Hudgins (Washington, D.C.: Cato Institute, 2000), pp. 152–56.

14. Campbell, "Modern Postal Reform Laws," p. 16.

15. Congress may wish to attach special conditions to ensure rural delivery in Alaska because such remote delivery may be an exceptional case.

16. One possible candidate for divestiture is the bulk mail system. See Adie, *Monopoly Mail*, p.136.

17. An example is the sale of the massive mail facility at Thirty-second Street and Eighth Avenue in Manhattan.

18. As noted, trucking deregulation created huge social benefits.

Index

Runyon, Marvin, 17, 26
Rural area customers, 3, 17, 99, 100, 117–18
    See also Cross-subsidization, Urban-rural cost differential

Salamon, Roger K., 48, 62
Salaries
    data description, 48–49, 131–32
    effect of reorganization on relative, 60–65
    See also Postal workers, salaries
Sales per postal worker, changes in, 64–68
Second-class mail, 48–49, 50t, 56–58, 133
Service workers' salaries, 63t, 64f
Shleifer, Andre, 20
Sidak, J. Gregory, 27, 45
Smith, Sharon P., 43
Spain, 114
Spulber, Daniel F., 27, 45
Stamps.com, 97
Standard mail A. *See* Third-class mail
Standard mail B. *See* Fourth-class mail
Stock prices, 78–79, 82
Supreme Court, 16, 40
Sweden, 3, 109, 118, 123, 125, 130
Switzerland, 112–13

Takeovers, 78, 80, 83
Taxpayer's equity, 34, 49, 71t, 72–73
Technological developments, 103–4, 127
    in communications, 2–3
    effects on USPS, 75, 95–104

and natural monopoly rationale, 101–3
Telecommunications, 87, 89t, 90t, 91t, 93t, 94t
Telephone, 99
Third-class mail, 56–58, 98–99, 134
Tierney, John T., 33, 38, 85
Tradable residual claims. *See* Transferable ownership shares
Transaction costs, 29–30
Transferable ownership shares, 75, 103, 127, 129–30
    and agency costs, 76–86
    role in postal reform, 117–19, 121
Trucking, 87, 89t, 90t, 91t, 92, 93t, 94t, 102

Unions, postal workers, 8–9, 43
United Kingdom, 114–15, 123
United Parcel Service, 20, 21, 28
United States Postal Service
    history of, 1–2, 14, 16–17, 96, 128
    See specific entries
United States Postal Service v. Council of Greenburgh Civic Associations, 16
Universal service, 15, 118, 130
    rationale and critiques of, 16–18, 20–22
    Urban-rural cost differences, 18–19, 29–30
    critiques of, 20–22
USPS. *See* United States Postal Service
Utility workers' salaries, 40–49, 51t, 63f, 64t

About the Author

Rick Geddes joined the Department of Policy Analysis and Management at Cornell University in the autumn of 2002. He was a national fellow at the Hoover Institution in 1999–2000. Mr. Geddes is an adjunct scholar at AEI. The author was an associate professor of economics at Fordham University from 1991 to 2002 and a visiting faculty fellow at Yale Law School in 1995.

His work has appeared in the *American Economic Review, Journal of Regulatory Economics, Encyclopedia of Law and Economics, Journal of Legal Studies, Journal of Law, Economics, and Organization,* and *Journal of Law and Economics.* In addition to postal economics, his research interests include the effects of regulation on corporate governance, public utility regulation, and the economics of women's rights.

Mr. Geddes holds MA and PhD degrees in economics from the University of Chicago and a BA from Towson State University in economics and finance.

Printed in the United States
18428LVS00004B/78

9 780844 741802